DREAMS
God's
FORGOTTEN
LANGUAGE

Also by John A. Sanford

THE KINGDOM WITHIN

DREAMS
God's
Forgotten
Language

by

john A. Sanford

J. B. LIPPINCOTT COMPANY
New York

STUDIES FROM THE C. G. JUNG INSTITUTE, ZURICH

88 89 90 91 92 20 19 18 17 16

ISBN–0–397–10056–6

Printed in the United States of America

Library of Congress Catalog Card No.: 68–29727

The original German edition has been made by Rascher Verlag, Zurich, under the title *Gottes vergessene Sprache*, edited by the Kuratorium of the C. G. Jung Institute, of Zurich.

To those who have helped guide me on the Way, and especially to Linny

preface
to the English Edition

This English edition of *Dreams: God's Forgotten Language*, which first appeared in a German translation in 1966, gives me a welcome opportunity to write a preface calling attention to the intent of this book and the frontiers of knowledge upon which it touches.

Dreams: God's Forgotten Language is primarily directed toward the intelligent layman; it tries to show, in as clear and simple a manner as possible, the relationship of dreams to religious experience. For this reason many of the examples I choose might strike the more experienced reader as ordinary. This is deliberate. My intention is not to go into the most complex dream material but to show the "extraordinary at work in the ordinary," i.e., to point out the spiritual overtones of meaning which are inherent in the simplest dreams of the most "ordinary" people among us.

I also want to make it quite clear that by referring to dreams as God's forgotten language I do not have in mind the "theological God" possessing a whole string of metaphysical attributes. By saying that our dreams are from God I mean that they are, from the point of view of the ego, purposively directed, and seem to revolve around a central authority in the psyche. There is always a creative element in dreams, and it is this creativity which is divine. It is the divine at work in the human soul with which I am concerned, not with elaborate creedal formulations.

I am so very indebted to the psychology of C. G. Jung for my understanding, and bring in so much of his psychological material, that in many ways this book may also serve as an introduction to Jung's psychology. I also hope, however, that some of the case material, formulations, and insight into Christian experience will prove original enough to interest even the reader already conversant with Jung.

In the last chapter of the book I bring up two problems which are each worthy of much more consideration than I have given them here. The problem of evil is only touched upon here and deserves much more study, and the question of dreams and a religious epistemology is vital. Since I was able to speak only briefly in this volume on this important subject, I am hoping to take it up again more completely in a second book.

Finally, the reader has my heartfelt wish that, if nothing else, he may finish the book with a little more feeling than he had before for the reality of the spiritual world. The metaphysical approach to life is "dead," and the modern mind no longer thinks in metaphysical terms. But spiritual reality is just beginning to be discovered. The world of the nonphysical, i.e., the world not apprehensible through our senses and which does not "occupy space," breaks in upon us in our dreams and in many other ways. It is this realm which carries to man's consciousness a revelation of the underlying meaning of life, and therefore of God. If this volume can add one bit more insight into the reality of this world I shall be well satisfied, and hope the reader will be too.

I would like to acknowledge with gratitude the help of Miss Helen Macey and Mrs. Ruth Budd with the preparation of this manuscript, and of my good friend George Doczi of Seattle, Washington, who rendered invaluable assistance in correlating the German and English editions.

JOHN A. SANFORD

iNTRODUCTION

This book is about dreams and religion, and in particular about the relevance of the dream to Christian experience. It is not a textbook on dream analysis, and many technical problems are passed over if they are not concerned with the main theme. Nor is this a textbook in psychology; though much Jungian psychology is discussed from time to time, this is not an attempt to outline Jung's teachings. Only as much psychology is introduced as is necessary to give the reader a feeling and insight into the religious function of the dreams that he has every night.

The plan of the book is simple. There are two parts. Part One has several chapters containing concrete examples of dreams drawn from my own counseling experience as a priest. The relevance of dreams for these pastoral counseling situations will be shown. Insofar as possible the dreams will be allowed to "speak for themselves," and there will be a minimum of technical interpretation. In Part Two the theological significance of dreams will be discussed more broadly. Here we will point out the role of dreams in the Bible and in the early Church; we will investigate the nature and structure of dreams, and we will elucidate what dreams have to say concerning the relationship of evil and the divine. We will conclude with our main argument, that dreams should rightly be regarded as God's forgotten language, or a Voice of God.

I am greatly indebted to those persons who permitted me

to discuss their dreams and stories. This is really their book. For their sakes, I have naturally used fictitious names and occasionally altered some minor details in their stories. In all other respects, the dreams and experiences are related as they happened.

For those who are unfamiliar with Jungian psychology, a brief definition of some basic terms will be helpful. "Ego" means the conscious part of personality. We are all of us aware of ourselves, we know what it is like to be awake and to fall asleep, we have a continuity of memory, and a certain capacity for making decisions and taking action. That part of us of which we are immediately aware, and which we usually identify as "I," is called the "ego." Strictly speaking, some parts of the ego are unconscious. But for our purposes we may call the ego our "consciousness." In our dreams our own person always represents the ego.

The "unconscious" refers to all those parts of our personality which we do not know. Freud long ago established the existence of unconscious personality components. Jung calls this part of the personality of which we are unaware "the unconscious." I do not use the word as though it referred to a definitely known and describable psychic entity, since our knowledge does not extend that far. The term "unconscious" is preferred to "subconscious" because the latter implies something below, hence inferior to, consciousness. As we shall see, the unconscious realm is just as much above the ego as it is below it; our higher spirituality is as much part of it as is our lower nature.

The "psyche" refers to the entire personality, including the ego and the unconscious: since the psyche embraces both, it is the term for the total psychological organism. "Psychic" is used as an adjective to describe the inner energy or activity of the psyche. "A dream is a psychic experience" means that it takes place within the psyche and not outside of it. It is not used in the way a spiritualist might use it, to describe some kind of supernatural communication.

CONTENTS

PART ONE

I

Agree with Thine Adversary

1

Seldom had I seen a more desperate situation. We were talking in Tom's bedroom. Tom was flat on his back in bed; I was sitting in a chair beside him. It was only in the middle of the afternoon but Tom looked tired and depressed. Hesitantly, piece by piece, he told me his story. Tom had been sick as a child and for many years he had been forced to keep to his bed. In time he had outgrown his childhood illnesses, and as a man he was vigorous and powerful. But now he was once again struck down with a disease which, if not arrested, would bring death within months, perhaps a year at the most. The only cure known to modern medicine was rest, rest, and more rest, and the support of a few drugs.

It was all very well to rest, Tom told me, but how could he possibly rest all the time? He was the sole means of support of his wife and children. In his job he was paid only when he worked. There was no set salary, no unemployment insurance, no sick leave. So how could he afford to rest?

I listened carefully, trying to put myself into his position. But what could I say? Anything I might utter about the goodness or love of God, or God's concern for him, would only sound like so many platitudes; it would only be cruel. Tom was up against some bitter facts. This was not the place for a sermon. Of course, we did talk some of God; it was Tom himself who introduced the subject. He told me how his own faith was all but gone, and how his wife vacillated between despair and prayers to God. He himself had had an unfortunate experience in his youth with a minister who betrayed his trust; this event had shaken his faith in people and in God. It was obviously a relief for Tom to speak frankly to someone who was not emotionally involved in the situation. Men have always found that they need each other to share the burdens of their soul. But there was a look of bewilderment and defeat in Tom's eyes which told me that in this case talking alone would not be enough.

Fortunately it was no accident that I was visiting Tom at this time, for his wife had phoned and asked me to come. It seems that some weeks before I had preached a sermon on dreams. I had pointed out that dreams tell us something today even as they once did to the men of the Bible. Willing to grasp at anything, Tom and his wife had decided to ask me to visit them. For Tom had noticed one thing about himself: he dreamed many dreams, and there were certain dreams which had returned again and again, for many years. I wondered if he had dreamed recently, and in reply he related the following simple dream of a few nights ago:

> I was in a room looking out of a small window at people who were playing golf. I wanted to go out to them but couldn't. The window was too small.

For centuries most men have disregarded dreams, and scoffed at their apparent absurdity. We know the usual attitude: "They just come from overeating, mere fragments left over from the day. . . . Just nonsense." But my own experience had been different. In the midst of my own

[*18*]

difficulties, it had been the understanding of my dreams which showed me the way through. Since then, my further studies of psychology and my experiences with the dreams of other people had opened up to me vast vistas of meaning. I began with the premise that dreams are facts. They exist, just as trees and rocks and birds exist. True, one cannot put them under the microscope, for they leave only a faint memory trace in our brain; they remain subjective, the personal business of the dreamer. Nevertheless, as events that take place in our world, they have as much right to careful study as any other event in nature. So far we haven't found anything in nature that doesn't have its function. So why should we say that of all created things the dream alone makes no sense?

Besides, in this case we were in no position to be choosy. There was nothing to be lost, and much to be gained, by making the assumption that Tom's dream made sense in a symbolic way. All of this we discussed. The question was how to get at the meaning of the dream.

Sigmund Freud, the first modern psychologist to explore the meaning of dreams, felt that dreams were a cover-up for something else; in other words that, underneath that which the dream seems to say, another meaning is hidden, which for various reasons cannot be spoken of directly. Dr. Jung has observed, however, that dreams are not obscure at all, but are clear expressions of our very own nature which mean exactly what they say. My own experience has convinced me of the correctness of Dr. Jung's position. The only difficulty is that dreams speak a symbolic language, and in order to understand them, one must understand their symbolism. One way to uncover the symbolism of a dream is for the dreamer to talk about it. It is, after all, *his* dream and has occurred in his psychic world, so it is reasonable to

[*19*]

assume that the dreamer himself might hold the clues to his dream's meaning. And so I asked Tom about golf and what it meant to him. Golf, Tom said, was his favorite game. He loved to play it and did so as often as possible. He deeply regretted that now his physical condition made it impossible for him to play. It reminded him of his childhood, when he could not play games but had to stay home, looking out the window and watching the other boys play.

What about being shut up in a room? It was of course very much like his present condition: it was being cooped up, unable to live. "But Tom," I said, "why didn't you go out of the room as you wanted to and join the game?" Tom's answer was like a flash of lightning illuminating the meaning of the dream: *"Because there was no door!"*

"Playing golf" means "living life." This is neither obscure nor difficult to understand. Tom had plainly said that playing golf meant health, enjoyment, and strength. But Tom couldn't live life, for he was shut up in a narrow, confined area; he could only look out of the window wistfully, as he used to do when he was a sick boy. He couldn't leave his place of confinement because the window was too small and there was no door. Windows are things people look out of; if we take the room as Tom's conscious world and the golf game going on outside as life, then the small window suggests: Tom's outlook on life is too small and narrow. With a larger outlook on life he might have been able to escape his confinement and find more freedom. Doors are things people go through to get in and out. The fact that there was no door to his room suggests that Tom, at that point in his life, had no way out of his predicament. So there was nothing unclear about the meaning of this dream. It meant exactly what it said in its own symbolic way: that Tom was shut up in his present condition and could not live life because he had no way out of his predicament.

We can look at it this way: if dreams have a meaning, it is clear that this meaning does not come from our conscious personality. And if we do not consciously make up our dreams out of our ego, out of that "I" part of us with which we are familiar, then the meaning of our dreams comes from an unconscious source of our psychic life. Suppose now that this unconscious part of our psyche has something to say to us. It cannot speak to us as we might talk to our neighbor over the fence. It must devise another means of communication: a symbolic language. By showing situations symbolically in dreams, the unconscious communicates with consciousness and discloses its own comments on the conditions of our life. This, at least, is our hypothesis. Now there is only one way to prove any hypothesis and that is to apply it to life experience and see if it works. In this case, when we apply this hypothesis to Tom's dream we find that symbolically, but directly and not obscurely, the dream is saying to Tom: you are shut up in your illness because your outlook on life is too narrow, and you have no door through which to escape.

All this I told Tom. He didn't greet my words with any rush of enthusiasm, but he could see that there might be some sense in them. I personally was encouraged by this dream for reasons I could not at the time explain to Tom. The dream suggested to me that Tom did not have to be sick! The only thing standing between him and life was the absence of a door. Tom, I decided, has not found a way out of this—as yet unknown—spiritual blind alley. I couldn't help but think of Christ's words, "I am the Way, the Truth, and the Life," and of his many allusions to being a "door." But what could this Way be, and how could it be found? I thought I knew the answer: the unconscious of his psyche and his dreams were themselves the way. Tom was trying to do everything only with his conscious mind. Enlisting the aid of the unconscious might open the door for him. So I told Tom as much as I thought I could, suggesting that the room in which he was shut up was only his own too narrow and limited conscious point of view, and that further dreams might "open a door." Tom was willing to try anything. We agreed that he would wait for further dreams and call me if they came. His situation looked as bleak as ever, but at least now he could look for a meaning to his experience.

A few days later I received a phone call. More dreams had come, and another appointment was set. The doctor permitted Tom to be up for a few hours each day, and this time Tom came to see me in my office. I was very curious what his new dreams were, but I shouldn't have been surprised to find they were nearly all variations of the same dreams he had had for so long before.

We have assumed that dreams may be meaningful. If this is so, then repeated dreams suggest that the unconscious psyche repeats the same message over and over. This message must be unusually important if it is so insisted upon. The reappearance of the oft-repeated dream in this case suggested that there was some spiritual or psychological problem which had been plaguing Tom for many years. Here is the dream:

> I saw myself in a warlike situation. Then a sinister adversary appeared. He had a gun or a knife. I fled but he pursued me and finally killed me.

What could we expect from this dream? Did this last dream contain anything that entitled us to hope? It seemed to speak only of darkness and death. Indeed the message is clear enough: something is trying to "kill" the dreamer. Now it only remains to ask, "Who is trying to kill the dreamer?" "What does it mean in a dream to die?" And, "Why does this take place?"

Let's first take Tom's enemy. Personality is a great deal more complex than it seems on the surface, and this complexity is reflected in the varying figures of our dreams. Characteristically we find ourselves in dreams repeatedly dealing with someone of our own sex who seems to be opposed, hostile, or inferior to us, someone of whom we are afraid, whom we despise. Who is this enemy? Ourself, of course! But it is not our accustomed conscious self who appears in this way as our enemy. It is rather an unconscious part of ourselves, something in us we do not want to face or recognize.

We have already used the hypothesis of an unconscious psychic reality to enable us to account for the origin of the dream. This same hypothesis also enables us to account for the existence of this adversary. It is hard for most of us to face ourselves. There is too much about which we feel guilty, which we do not wish to remember, too many weaknesses we want to avoid, and too many unpleasant memories we do not want to recall. So we simply banish these disagreeable things and pretend they do not exist. This does not at all mean they cease to be, they simply are repressed, but continue to live in the unconscious like another person. This "other person" appears in our dreams so regularly he has been given a name. Jung calls him "the shadow." The first part of the dream could hardly be more clear: "Tom is at war with himself. He is afraid of his shadow, the unknown in himself, and runs away." Furthermore, since Tom has had such a dream for many years, it is an old problem and not a new one.

What about the death of the dreamer? To Tom this was

only another reason to believe that he was actually going to die. Now death might mean extinction. But it might also mean transformation. Men have always suggested the idea of profound transformation through the symbols of death and resurrection. It really is quite clear: nothing can change unless the old dies in order that the new shall be. This is the Mystery at the heart of Christianity: the death of Christ leads to resurrection. The Bible is filled with language which describes transformation of personality as the death of the old Adam and the birth of the new. Not for nothing did St. Paul say, "I die daily." Perhaps then "to die" equals "to change."

The idea of death as a symbol of transformation also offers an answer to our third question, "Why does the adversary want to kill the dreamer?" It may be that this shadow is intent upon radically transforming Tom. It would be better if Tom would face himself so that he would "die unto himself," voluntarily undergoing a transformation of his personality. But if necessary the transformation will be forced upon him by the unconscious.

Looked at this way there is nothing vague about this dream. It speaks in a symbolic but understandable language, using war, conflict, an adversary, and death, in order to convey its message. We may sum up its meaning: "You are involved in inner conflict and are running away from yourself. You must die unto yourself and be born again. But if you try to escape from your problem, you will be overtaken by it violently."

This was our hypothesis about the dream's meaning. I was sure in my heart about this meaning, but then I had the benefit of having experienced thousands of dreams and learned from them the kind of language they use. For Tom, however, this was a venture of faith. Nevertheless, it did provide a way for him to think about his situation, which opened up wide vistas of further significance. For if this were the meaning of the dream, then it was possible that everything that was happening to Tom was part of a plan, that "something within him" was intent upon his transformation, and if Tom persisted in avoiding this spiritual transformation it would be forced upon him through his illness. These, at least, were hypotheses we could not help but consider. Our later experience bore out their truth.

If I were to go into all the dreams, conversations, and ups and downs which we shared during our counseling it would take a book in itself. The course of events was by no means smooth. At first, as soon as Tom had gotten in touch with his dreams and had related them to his inner life, there was an immediate and noticeable improvement in his physical condition. Within a short time he was permitted by his doctor to resume part of his work load. During this time the dreams continued to flow with symbolism which was quite fascinating and very complex. The central problem continued to be the problem of the shadow, the dark and dreadful "someone" in himself, and I was uneasy that this problem continued to persist so long.

Then finally there came a time of great tension and anxiety, a return of all the old physical symptoms, and a frantic trip back to the doctor. Was all our work to be for nothing? Were we to wind up worse off than before? It proved, however, to be the last violent resistance in the painful process of self-recognition. Soon after this Tom related the tragic tale of his past and freed himself of the fear that his part in a bitter experience would be exposed by someone who knew of it. Then I realized for the first time the terrible fear in which he had been living. I am not at liberty to relate the details. He had, however, reason to be afraid that his past might be exposed to those who trusted him. During this time of inner conflict and confession his physical condition remained critical, but there was no choice now; all had to be seen through to the end. It was Tom himself who decided to make an honest confession with those concerned. Only in this way, Tom decided, could he live free from fear. It was like going to the dentist: taking out a sick tooth is painful, but when it is over then the fear is over too. With spiritual courage Tom set his personal relationships straight, and made his peace with those involved. Almost immediately, his physical condition improved markedly. Then came this following most interesting dream:

> Again I was in a warlike situation. My enemy again approached me with a knife. He wanted to kill me. I started to run, but then I stopped and, facing him, said instead, "All right, kill me if you want to." The enemy also stopped and paused. *Then he smiled and, turning, walked away.*

In the light of what we have said previously, this dream's interpretation is simple. Again the shadow appears, again he threatens with violence. But this time Tom turns to face himself, and voluntarily consents to the terrors of "death." The purpose of the shadow has been accomplished; by turning and consenting to his "death," Tom takes his transformation upon himself. "Murder" is now no longer necessary. The shadow smiles, turns, and walks away.

There is a Biblical parallel to these dreams so striking that I mention it here: it is the story of Jacob's wrestling with his adversary.[1] At the urging of God, Jacob has left the land of his uncle, Laban, to which he had fled from fear of his brother Esau, whom Jacob had cheated out of his father's blessing. Now he stands at the stream Jabbok, the border line between his own country and the land of Laban, and so the point of no return. On the other side of the stream lives his estranged brother Esau, whom he will surely encounter the next day if he crosses the stream. Jacob sends his family and servants ahead and spends the night alone with his own thoughts. We may well imagine the guilt, the fear, the doubts about God's guidance which assailed him. And we are told that "a man" came in the night and wrestled with him. But Jacob accepted the struggle, and wrestled so hard that as the sun rose his assailant said to him, "Let me go, for the day is breaking." But Jacob replied, "I will not let you go, unless you bless me." With that the assailant declared, "Your name shall no more be called Jacob, but Israel [meaning 'one who wrestles with God'], for you have striven with God and have prevailed." [2]

Jacob's adversary is himself; psychologically we could say his shadow, the other man in him, the fear, guilt, and doubt from which he had run away. But this shadow is in the service of God, and to wrestle with this other one in us is also to wrestle with God! The result is a transformation of personality, represented in the story by the change of name from Jacob to Israel. In Biblical days a man's name expressed his nature; to know a person's name was to know his inner being. (That is the reason why in verse 29 the divine assailant does not tell Jacob his own name!) Thus Jacob is Jacob no longer, but Isra-el (a wrestler with God): No more is he the self-centered, clever schemer who cheated his brother Esau. He is now Israel, the Father of his people.

Now it doesn't matter at this point whether the reader believes in the Bible as historical fact or not. As far as our present purposes are concerned, the only important thing is that this Biblical story is rich with psychological meaning.

[27]

Whether it actually happened that way, or is only an oral tradition, it nevertheless expresses a psychological truth as true today as in Jacob's day: that God assails us in our life as our shadow, seeming to be an adversary, but desiring our fundamental change. A story like this which is typical of oft-repeated psychological situations we call "archetypal."

Let us return to Tom. After this dream, his physical condition immediately and swiftly improved. The counseling continued, and in six months he was back at work fully recovered. Had this problem not been dealt with, Tom would probably be dead today, for his physical sickness was not imaginary but quite real. Tom's dreams led him into the only way he could follow to regain his health. They led like a thread from the labyrinth of his own thoughts to renewed healthy attitudes, to a free conscience, and to reconstructed relationships. We may therefore assume an intelligence within his psyche, responsible for these meaningful dreams. For reasons which will appear more clearly as we go on, I do not hesitate to call this intelligence "God." God is the name men give to the purposeful, numinous power which crosses our lives; our dreams are one of the manifestations of this power.

Someone might question, "Is it not dangerous to deal with God so directly, if He is the author of our dreams?" The answer is, "Yes, it is dangerous." In Tom's case the risk was warranted, since nothing could have been more dangerous than his present situation. Even Tom found that dealing with the unconscious material his dreams related was not easy, but an exacting and demanding task. Not without reason does man fear God, for who knows when He may want to make a Moses out of us, send us on some impossible inner task, and threaten us with destruction if we try to evade Him? If one expects in dealing with dreams to find the beneficent, fuzzy-minded Deity of much conventional religion he will be greatly surprised. The Author of our dreams is a demanding Deity. He leads, but also demands; He helps and renews our strength, but He can also be inexorable in the tasks which He expects us to accomplish. I insert this warning here, for if the reader is looking for an easy way out, he will not want to deal with unconscious psychic reality. Yet, not only for Tom, but also for most of us, it is less dangerous to deal with Him directly than to compel Him to thrust us forcibly into the way He sets before us.

2

The story of Tom is unusual. Not everyone has the deeply buried problem Tom had, yet all of us dream, and our dreams always have a meaningful message. That all of us dream is a fact based upon scientific evidence.[3] By observing movements under a sleeper's eyelids and by means of the electroencephalogram, it is possible for scientists to determine whether or not the sleeper is dreaming. One of the scientists who have made intensive experiments in this area, Dr. William Dement, assures us that all people dream several times a night whether or not they remember their dreams.[4] We will have occasion later to refer to these experiments in more detail. As for the assertion that all dreams have meaning, this the reader must for the moment assume with me. In dealing with thousands of dreams I have not yet found a single aimless or meaningless one. Moreover, it would be careless to assume that some dreams reveal deep wisdom while others are sheer nonsense, for this would be like assuming that some physical bodies obey the law of gravity but others do not. Some of our dreams appear to be obscure only because we do not understand their symbolic meaning.

To illustrate the meaningful nature of the dreams of "ordinary" people, I would like to present the following example. The woman who was consulting me had no pressing problem. In fact, had she not consulted me earlier on other matters, she probably would not have brought this difficulty to my attention at all. She was of middle age, alert, capable, and very honest with herself; she was well-liked and a woman of exceptional character. But in everybody's life there are certain things which seem very important, things on which we base our feeling of security; a threat to these things produces anxiety. Her security rested upon her work and upon the admiration and respect she received at her job. She was in fact a very capable woman, with an excellent administrative position, and highly regarded by her profession. For some time now, however, she had been discontented with this work, feeling that she was spending too much time in administration and not dealing sufficiently with people. But when a change did come in her work she found herself ill-prepared to accept it. The department was reorganized completely, heads rolled, and those employees who were retained were reshuffled.

In this process Louise (as we shall call her) was given a new assignment in which she would be dealing with people much more than before, but would have less to do with administrative paper work. The salary was the same, the responsibility as great, but the title was less impressive. In one way it was what she had hoped for, but in another way she felt threatened by the change, fearful of a loss of status, anxious lest she be forced to think less of herself. Like many of us, she cared more for status symbols and for the opinions of other people than for her own sense of values.

She identified herself with her position in life and not with her real self. So she lost connection with parts of her nature which seemed not to fit into the picture of "the important woman," and, in so doing, she lost much that was really valuable in her whole personality. In the midst of this little crisis, the kind that might happen to any of us, she brought me this dream:

> The dream began with a white woman about my age and size who resembled my mother-in-law; she argued with another person whom I could not see, presumably myself. During the argument the visible woman slowly changed into a very dark woman; her dress was plain, buttoned down the front, like the uniform of a maid. I was annoyed by this colored woman standing in front of me, and said: "Go on back to your bed and stay there. I do not want you! Maybe I will see you tomorrow." The scene changed; suddenly I was in my back yard, and it was quite dark or dusky, presumably early in the morning. The yard was untidy, littered with empty wooden boxes (like orange crates) and a large amount of small wood, such as that used in fireplaces. I was trying to bring about order by stacking the wood and the boxes. The same dark, colored woman appeared before me again saying, "I can work, please let me try." I was unhappy about her appearance and said, "I don't think it will work; go away." The dark woman just stood there looking at me with steady eyes. A man's voice, strong and quiet, came to me distinctly, "Why don't you let her try?" I did not see the man, but there was no doubt; it was a man's voice. Then I awoke.

This is a long dream with many details. These details also play their part in the dream, but for our purposes we shall discuss only the main points. (The male figure whose voice speaks in the dream is, for example, the dreamer's animus, to be discussed later.)

The main element in the dream is the encounter between the dreamer and a menial servant woman. The dreamer does not want the help or even the presence of this servant woman, but the latter wants very much to assist. If we reject our dreams, then we can just close the books on messages such as this. But this is an experiment in which we try to give dreams a chance to speak to us. So being both sporting and scientific, we ask the crucial question, "Who is the servant woman?" She is not another actual human being, nor is she a figment of imagination. If she has reality, then her reality is to be found within the dreamer herself. We are justified in surmising that the servant woman represents something about the dreamer's own personality. She could be just what she appears to be: that part of the dreamer which seems to her inferior and menial, in short, her shadow. Now this hypothesis brings us rich rewards, for we know from the woman's actual life that she was feeling anxious at the time because of a threat to her status, fearing that she would be placed in an apparently inferior position. She is afraid because she cannot accept that side of herself which is simple and down-to-earth: the "servant."

Tom's shadow seemed threatening and dangerous, but only as long as he was ignored, for in reality he was in the service of the development of Tom's personality. Louise's shadow, though unwanted and inferior, has just those capacities and attitudes which are necessary to save the situation. As the servant says: she wants to be put to work! One should take this quite literally: the time has come for Louise to employ in her work her own seemingly inferior side, to really get down and *serve* people. In ignoring this serving side of herself, Louise has suppressed one of her very best qualities.

[*32*]

Thus it is no coincidence that Louise has such a positive shadow. The positive nature of the servant woman in the dream comes from the dreamer's sincere efforts to straighten up her back yard. All of us have walked along a street looking at the nice, neat front yards of houses. But if we walked up the alley we might get a different impression. There might be trash cans, unmowed lawns, and littered corners. It doesn't take much imagination to see that the "back yard" is the dreamer's own inner back yard, the side of herself most people don't get to see. We keep the front yard tidy for the sake of appearances; the backyard we keep in order for the sake of God! In the dream, the dreamer is not ready to accept her shadow fully, but she at least makes an effort to get her inner life in order. The shadow always turns to us the face we turn to him. As long as Tom feared his shadow and ran, the shadow was dreadful; when Tom turned and faced him, the shadow smiled. Because Louise makes a sincere effort to deal with her back yard, she finds her shadow eager to cooperate and to help.

It was Louise's honesty and intelligence which made her see the truth of her dream. She acted upon it and found that not only the public, but all of her department, came to rely upon her more and more. Her status now is greater than ever before. But more than that: having accepted her inferior side, her shadow, she no longer needs the status symbol of her position; of this she is truly free!

3

St. Peter had his doubts, St. Thomas his incredulity, Elijah in the wilderness his despair, Christ on the Cross his feeling of being forsaken by God. No one has so much faith that there is no doubt in him; no one has such purity that he has no darkness. Within every human attribute there hides somewhere its opposite.

We usually ignore this truth; we insist upon a one-sided personality, and then become its victim. Chief among these victims is the typical American minister today, who is constantly in danger of falling prey to preconceived ideas of what a clergyman is like. I should know, for I am one myself. Think of what a minister must do all week: write sermons about faith, show forth in his life goodness, love, and kindness, offer up to suffering humanity hope and healing. But what about his own doubts, his own hatred, the evil in him, and his own despair? As anyone knows who really has known clergymen, the minister is no more free of these tendencies than other people. In fact, the devils of hell can pursue him all the more hotly just because he is a clergyman.

The next dream comes from the story of a young minister who was almost destroyed by this problem. Carefully educated and filled with zeal, he identified himself with goodness, faith, love, and comforting words. His difficulties began one night when he awoke in terror with the desperate sensation that he was wrestling with the devil himself. It seemed as though all the forces of evil were in the room with him, and it was only with great difficulty that he calmed himself. From that night on his anxieties were great, and eventually he went to someone for help.

We have perhaps already glimpsed enough of the way dreams work to realize that his first dreams were of terrible, dark, and dangerous people. He was meeting his own shadow, his own dark side, which simply would not fit into the image of the perfect priest and so had been repressed. Interesting things happened as the young clergyman recognized that the "devil"—all that was hateful, doubting, and disturbing—was in himself. The recognition of these dark parts of himself in no way took away his effectiveness as a priest. In fact, only when he knew something of what it was like to be a human being could he really help others!

This man had many interesting dreams, but I wish to dwell upon only one, which occurred later in his development. Naturally the problem of his own shadow was likely to become more acute when his work seemed to force him to identify completely with goodness, faith, and love. One particularly dangerous time, for instance, is Easter week, when a clergyman is busy late into the night with his ministry and preaching. Our other side by no means ceases to exist during Easter week; it simply carries on its activities in the unconscious, creating its own kind of mischief. This particular Easter, however, the priest was forewarned, and determined to keep "in touch" with himself. He knew by now how doubting, cynical, and unfeeling he could be, and he never forgot it. During this Easter week he dreamed the following dream:

> I am in my clericals and go to an old store and enter. The proprietor looks at me strangely. I read the menu (there is a restaurant section). It is around noontime. Then some rough-looking people about my own age enter and sit with me at a round table. One of them in particular looks at me. I recognize this particular person; it seems I know him well from some previous encounter. We are so dissimilar: I a minister—he a beatnik. He asks me if I recognize him and I say I do. We talk at some length. He tells me he has lied to me before, he really does not work. Instead he spends much time fishing at the beach.

For our purposes it is sufficient to deal with the main theme of the dream and leave aside the details. This main

theme is the encounter of the priest-dreamer and the beatnik at the round table. Who is this beatnik? We can't help
but see the similarity with Tom's enemy and Louise's servant; the beatnik must be the minister's shadow. The contrast is startling. The minister must present to the world the
traditional faith and morality of the Church, and the great
concern of the Church for people. He also must work very
hard. The beatnik is the direct opposite: he has discarded
traditional faith and morality and does not work at all!
They are in the dream like the elder and the prodigal son!
Priest or not, every human being has two sides; neither side
can deny the other and escape the consequences.

The interesting thing about this dream, however, is the
relationship which exists between the two. The minister sits
down, the beatnik joins him. Then he asks the crucial
question: "Do you recognize me?" And the minister can
truthfully answer, "Yes." This is always the key question
with the shadow: do we recognize him? The recognition
established, the minister and beatnik do not harm each other
but engage in fruitful conversation. They are in fact, related together in the context of the whole personality. We
cannot say, "The real personality is the minister," or, "The
real personality is the beatnik." The real, whole personality
includes and transcends both.

We have seen ego and shadow as parts of one personality. What might symbolize the wholeness of personality
that transcends both ego and shadow? What is the unity
which embraces both sides? Is there anything in this dream
which might suggest such a transcending wholeness? Yes:
the table around which the two are seated. A table unites
those who sit around it. It stands as a symbol for the spiritual unity of those who belong together. In certain countries
to eat together means to establish friendship. Even Christ at

the Last Supper gathered with His disciples around a table, as Christians still do symbolically when they partake of the Eucharist.

In this case, the table as a symbol of the unity between the dreamer and his shadow is reinforced by its shape: it is expressly described as a circle. Suppose you or I wanted to represent in a geometric figure the idea of wholeness, unity, or totality: what more distinct symbol could we use than that of the square or circle? Both of these shapes have balance and harmony: the square because each side is equal in length to the other sides, the circle because all its points are equidistant from the center. And in fact, we will find in religions all over the world that the circle and square reappear again and again as symbols of wholeness. We will have occasion later to talk further about such symbols. They are especially important because their origin lies not in the individual personality but in a deeper layer of human nature that all men share in common. This deeper layer Jung calls "The Collective Unconscious."

We can now summarize: the dreamer is so hard at work being a Christian minister that he is in special danger of losing touch with himself and becoming split into two people, one conscious and the other unconscious. The dream reminds the dreamer of the two sides of himself and shows the vital connection existing between them. United they are greater than if each lived separately only for himself.

There is one other aspect of this dream, a bit humorous, but also profound, which I cannot resist calling attention to. The beatnik expressly says that he does not work, but spends his day fishing at the beach! This is obviously in deliberate contrast to the minister who is working too much. But who knows, the beatnik may actually catch a fish in the ocean! And the fish from time immemorial has had special significance as a psychological symbol.⁵ The fish is a living creature which lurks in the depths where it cannot be seen, and so stands for a vital unconscious content. In our early Christian era, the fish was also a symbol for Christ Himself. The dream then points to this strange paradox: that our shadow has a vital place in our psychic life. He is not just someone to be despised, because he actually "fishes up" for us exactly what we need.

Summary

I have presented five dreams from the lives of three people. In doing so I have merely touched upon human nature and its problems, and the interpretation of these dreams might seem a bit arbitrary to the reader who has no experience with dream material. In an empirical study such as this, only familiarity with many thousands of dreams can give us a firm basis of knowledge. If we had seen only a few daffodils we could not be sure that daffodils were always yellow-white. If however we had seen thousands of daffodils we could be justified in the assumption that "all daffodils are yellow-white," though of course there is always theoretically the chance that some day a blue daffodil might turn up. After looking at thousands of dreams and seeing certain typical patterns and structures, we can with some confidence say: this dream figure looks like the dreamer's shadow. If the future dreams and course of therapy bear out the assumption, then we can assume that the interpretation is on solid ground. But to someone turning to dreams for the first time it might not seem that apparent. Someone seeing his first daffodil might say, "How do you know they are always that color?" To make up for this difficulty I have tried to be as logical as possible; for dreams have their own logic, and dream symbols are inherently reasonable.

These five dreams had the problem of the shadow as their common denominator. In Tom's case we saw the shadow as Tom's deadly enemy, until finally Tom made peace with him. In Louise's case, we saw the shadow as a positive, though rejected, potentiality within her. In the case of the minister we saw the possibilities of a creative solution to the shadow problem.

The problem of the shadow has only recently been formulated in psychological language by C. G. Jung. But it is a problem as old as mankind. In literature we can see an excellent example of the shadow problem in Robert Louis Stevenson's *Dr. Jekyll and Mr. Hyde* and also in his less well-known work, *The Master of Ballantrae*. In the Bible there are many examples of the two opposite sides of human nature which must be reconciled: Cain and Abel, Jacob and Esau, Mary and Martha, the Elder Son and the Prodigal, and many more. In history, the problem of the shadow is disastrously apparent, for always men have talked of good and wrought evil. Christian nations war on each other, men accuse each other of evil they intend to do themselves, social injustice persists, and superficial espousal of Christianity is no preventive. In World War II man's shadow burst out in full rage, as seemingly Christian nations became possessed by the demonic evil that is inherent in human nature and becomes so destructive when it is not recognized. And today, we all stand in fear of one thing: that our unrecognized, unredeemed shadow will start another frightful catastrophe. We all talk peace but prepare for war. Obviously, human nature has two sides, and it is difficult to reconcile them. Accusing our neighbor of possessing those qualities we hate and fear so much in ourselves is no help in solving the problem.

[39]

Consequently, it is of considerable importance that our dreams are concerned with this problem and how to deal with it, for our dreams contain a real teaching about the shadow. In the five dreams we have discussed we can summarize this teaching as follows:

1. The shadow is a reality. If we deny our own seemingly evil or inferior side, we only drive it into the unconscious, where it carries on its own peculiar life and becomes doubly dangerous. To remain unaware of our true nature solves nothing. This only makes the problem worse because it permits the shadow to operate autonomously from the unconscious without relationship to the whole personality.

2. By showing us this shadow, our dreams compensate our conscious attitudes. We have a certain conscious picture of ourselves; the dreams show our nature in a different light. If we consider this it will be less likely that we intend good and do evil.

3. Our dreams also tell us that our shadow is by no means without value. Tom's shadow actually was working in the service of his growth. Louise's shadow was just what she needed. The minister's shadow went fishing. The shadow, feared and rejected, becomes evil. Recognized and accepted he plays his part in the total man. Our dreams show us that the darker, weaker part of our personality also has an important role to play in the drama of our wholeness.

4. Dreams thus introduce another concept to our understanding of human nature: they reveal to us that there is something of importance beyond the ego. The total man is more than just that portion of the personality which the ego represents.

The inclusion of the shadow into the total personality, in which everything plays its part, is possible. This concept was only hinted at in the dreams of this chapter. But I mention it now, for it will appear again as the thread which goes through all our dreams. If there really is a unity which binds together ego and shadow, then this is of the utmost importance. It is exactly this unity we must find if the world is to escape disaster. If the human shadow, unrecognized and resentful, breaks loose once more he now has terrible weapons at his command!

The facts I have presented in this chapter tell us that dreams are not "nonsense" but intelligible communications of vital things. We cannot say that this shadow problem is just a matter for psychology, nor can we claim that this is only a moral problem for religion. The problem of the shadow demands both psychological insight and spiritual perspective, if it is to be solved. At the level of the dream, psychology and religion are inseparable.

Jesus Christ said, "Agree with thine adversary quickly, while thou art in the way with him." Men have always believed Jesus was talking merely about an unfriendly neighbor. Our dreams say that he was referring to our inner adversary, with whom we can fortunately come to an agreement and so be at peace with ourselves. In fact, until we have peace with this inner adversary, peace with our neighbors will be impossible, since we will always blame them for what is in us. It makes no difference at this point whether or not the reader accepts the historical figure of Jesus. The advice "agree with thine adversary" remains, psychologically and spiritually, profoundly important.

It is high time the churches talked less about conscious commitment to ideals and creeds, and more about what to do with that living reality, our shadow. And it would be good if we clergy spent less time as ivory-tower theologians and more as doctors of the soul. Perhaps God doesn't know

[41]

He was supposed to have stopped talking with men when they closed the canon of the New Testament! He may never have been informed that His revelation is ended, and so He is still speaking to us in our dreams today! If so, then one thing He says to us is: "Christian, make peace with your adversary." We would do well to listen.

II

Though Your Sins Are Like Scarlet

"It happened many years ago, but facing it now it is as real as if it were yesterday." The woman before me, whom we will call Margaret, was alert, anxious, middle-aged. As she spoke I could reconstruct the picture in my mind: an unhappy, immature girl, married too young, burdened with the weight of a wretched childhood. The childhood story was cruel. First there had been quarrels between her father and mother and finally divorce while the little girl was yet very small. Then there had been a living lie as the mother remarried, but passed off the stepfather as the real father. Later there came abuses from the stepfather, and finally the realization by the child of the lie that had been foisted on her. A father who was not her own, a mother who had never really wanted her and had lied to her: the result, an unhappy, resentful young human being. Then came the early marriage, much too soon, just an attempt to escape from her unhappiness, a marriage which lasted but a short time. But within this short marriage the unhappy girl, over-taken by yet another extraordinary and cruel trick of life which I am not at liberty to divulge, committed what was to her a terrible sin.

But Margaret had a great deal of courage and determination. To be sure, she could not tell anyone of this black deed—with good reason she distrusted people—but she could bury the deed firmly, forget it, and go on in life. And go on she did, with considerable success. She chose a profession, worked hard, and became successful. She remarried and was for a short while actually happy for the first time in her life. Then her second husband died, the first man (except perhaps her actual father from early childhood) whom she had loved.

But recovering, she remarried again. This time the marriage lasted, though she had to stick through many difficult years with her husband when he became ill. Everyone would have said, "Here is a woman who can be proud of herself and her achievements." No one knew of her unhappy childhood. No one knew of the dark deed she had succeeded in repressing so completely.

It is curious how people come to talk about themselves. Sometimes it begins with something quite remote. Then a conversation opens up, a feeling of trust is established for some unknown reason, and often scarcely realizing it someone may begin to unburden his heart. So it was that Margaret first came with a minor problem seemingly unrelated to the deeper burdens of her soul. But something within her which she herself did not understand was crying out for understanding and release, and she spoke, for the first time in her life, of the unhappiness at the bottom of her heart and the darkness of the deed which she had done.

So often when we first unburden our souls to another human being, there takes place an emotional release which the psychotherapists call "catharsis." It is an extraordinarily healing experience. In fact, if we have never experienced catharsis, our life is not complete. But in this case, the release was not forthcoming. I was concerned; the burden of guilt was not lifted, but seemed to increase. Perhaps it was because it had been buried so deeply in the unconscious, so far down that Margaret herself scarcely realized it was there. So when the lid was lifted off and the guilt came rolling forth it seemed to grow and grow in intensity, like water breaking through a dam.

There are times when all one can do for someone is to stand by patiently while the other goes through an unavoidable crisis of the soul. But what would bring release? Should I preach to her, and tell her of the everlasting forgiveness of God? But this she knew, at least intellectually; she had heard it in sermons a hundred times before. The only thing I could do for her was to show her, without many words, that I took her and her business seriously and that I believed that forgiveness could somehow be possible. It was at this point that Margaret dreamed the following dream, and then a short time later, a second one.

The first dream:

I was in a fairly large square room; the room was dark, or perhaps dusky or shadowy would be a better description. I was sitting on the floor against the wall opposite the only door, which seemed closed. In the center of the room was a well or tubular iron shaft. The opening was even with the floor and seemed approximately twenty-four inches in diameter; in any event, probably too small for me to get into. I crept on my hands and knees slowly over to the well and looked into it. At first I saw nothing but darkness and what seemed to be unlimited depth; however, soon (seconds perhaps) a square piece of white paper about eight by eight inches came into view. It was slowly floating downward in this very deep well or hole. The paper could easily be seen to be blank, as it appeared to be lighted or fluorescent. Although it seemed to be a well, there was no water, at least none was visible. I felt afraid and crawled back against the wall. Almost immediately my little Boston terrier dog appeared at the opposite side of the room; presumably he came through the door. He looked at me and walked directly toward the well. Instead of coming to me, however, he turned his tail toward me and jumped into the well without a sound being uttered. I screamed for my husband, or thought that I screamed. This must have wakened me.

The second dream:

About one week after we returned from vacation I had the following very short but deeply impressive dream. I remember nothing except looking upward (either lying on my back or standing up) and seeing a shower of white square papers, about eight by eight inches, float down close to me. It seemed they were descending directly to me or upon me, although I did not touch them. The papers seemed to be very white, obviously blank, and they seemed to be lighted in some way. As I look back on the dream the paper seemed to float down noiselessly and gracefully like snow. This dream seemed in no way unpleasant."

Margaret made certain remarks in connection with these dreams. The well or iron shaft was a frightening thing. As a well it did not seem to contain water, but to lead into the earth. She was terribly afraid of it. Her little dog was much loved by her, a friendly household pet. She described her fear in the first dream, her reluctance to peer into the well. In the second dream she noted the striking similarity between the many sheets of white paper and the one sheet of paper in the first dream. But in the second dream the fear was gone.

There are three main ingredients in the first dream: the well or iron shaft, the paper, and the dog. If we could understand the meaning of these figures the dream would become clear. Let's begin with the well. The well is something which goes into the earth. Just as the sky is thought of as heaven, and is associated in our minds with the Heavenly

Father, so the earth is the realm of the "Earth Mother," where things and people are buried and put away. For centuries men have regarded the depths of the earth as the "lower" world, the world of infernal and unknown things, the location of hell, and the final burying place of the body. Of course, it is the same earth which brings forth life and fruit, but at this moment only the sinister associations are apparent. The dream uses the earth to symbolize the unknown, dark unconscious realm, in contrast to the ordinary, conscious world above ground. The well or shaft in the center of the room says that these depths are now in the center of things. The suggested image is that the depths must be looked into, perhaps even entered. But at this moment the fear is too great.

Now perhaps the reader may have noticed something. In describing the well and the earth I have made use of allusions, such as to hell, which are common to mankind everywhere. In myths, religions, and dreams the world over, the earth means the precipitous, the unfathomable, as much as it means the fruitbearing source of life. In talking about hell and graves I am using associations which are not the personal product of Margaret's individual mind but have a well-nigh universal significance. The reason is this: we are dealing here with a layer of Margaret's psyche which goes beyond her own personal experience in life, into those fundamental layers of the psyche which are universal. We mentioned earlier in connection with the dream of the young minister that the circle as a symbol of totality came from such unconscious layers, and that Jung named this dimension of the psyche the "Collective Unconscious."

When we come to the next symbol, the square piece of white, luminous paper, this collective, or archetypal, element will be even more apparent. Margaret herself could not imagine what this paper meant, except that its whiteness and blankness suggested to her something clean and unwritten upon. However, the square and circle, as we found earlier, have frequently been associated with the idea of man's totality. And luminosity suggests that this squareness, this totality, is not just a dead concept, but a living psychic reality of radiant power.

Now for the dog. The dog is of course a domesticated animal. An animal is instinctive. It possesses little if any conscious reasoning ability but acts solely upon instinct or unreflecting nature. Margaret's own favorite animal is instinctively associated with her. The dog in our dreams frequently has a saving significance, taking instinctively the right direction or the right action in times when our conscious minds might have hesitated. An example may be seen for instance in the children's story *The Wizard of Oz*. Here the rescue of Dorothy and her friends is accomplished through the instinctive, impulsive efforts of her little dog.

The whiteness of the paper suggests cleanness and freshness; the square shape suggests wholeness and totality. It comes down from above, that is from the realms of heaven, and thus suggests something of a higher origin. Putting these things together I suggested to Margaret that the paper was a symbol of her own life, which was now cleansed, whitened, ready to be written upon once more, and given back to her from above as a *tabula rasa*, though still in a paperlike rather than vital form. If this were so, then the meaning of the dream is clear: "the hope for a renewed and whole life has come down from on high."

This saving power, however, does not lead away from her own depths, but into it. The highest descends into the lowest. And though she is afraid, something deeply instinctive in her, without hesitation, is willing to rush into the depths in pursuit, presumably, of the wholeness the paper suggests. I was reminded of the words of Isaiah, and quoted them to her: "Come now, let us reason together, says the Lord: though your sins are like scarlet, they shall be as white as snow; though they are red like crimson, they shall become like wool." [1]

I wish I could say that Margaret was immediately released from her guilt after this dream and our interpretation. But such was not the case, for her fear was too great. That was why the second dream came. And in this dream there was a whole shower of square, white, luminous pieces of paper. It is as though the dream was determined to draw Margaret's attention to the reality of her forgiveness, to the fact that her life now really was cleansed. Indeed, does not the insistence of this dream with its whole shower of white papers touch us as almost humorous?

The persistence of her dreams impressed Margaret: this time the restoration was accomplished and her guilt was banished.

A short time later Margaret had a sequel to these dreams. Again she was standing by a dark well, looking over the edge. This time the well was large enough to permit her to enter, but her fear prevented her from descending. Then a man appeared and, without a word, shoved her over. Down she fell, expecting to be drowned in the depths, but lo: she landed painlessly on solid ground and found herself in a beautiful garden. With this dream her fears were greatly reduced. This dream needs no interpretation, except for the presence of the man, who might be a reference to the counselor, upon whose urging she had perhaps moved into the depths faster than she had anticipated. But no longer was the unconscious a dreadful abyss; it was now a beautiful garden.

[49]

This dream was a real experience. It showed the depths and heights of a spiritual world which go beyond our personal life. It demonstrates that the unconscious is not just a basement [2] into which we repress objectionable facts, but a living reality which, together with consciousness, works toward a goal which seems to include healing and wholeness. But the dream also has a special message for the Christian: a message about forgiveness. Of all the things that the Cross stands for, forgiveness is one of the most prominent. But forgiveness is a work of the soul, an inner experience which must be gone through. And the first thing required from us is the recognition of the depths of our own guilt.

Every churchgoer has been taught that God forgives sins and that Christ died on the Cross to lift the burden of guilt from us; yet few feel in their heart actually forgiven and free. This becomes immediately apparent when we uncover the unconscious realm of the psyche. When we observe the wide gulf between our Christian message and the actual human situation we must ask ourselves: "What is wrong?"

The problem often begins with the lack of recognition of our guilt. For today it is no longer fashionable to feel guilty. Too many "easy-going" Christians have told us: it isn't necessary to feel guilty any more because God just wipes it all away as fast as we accumulate it. And on the other hand certain psychologists tell us it is foolish to feel guilty; this is supposed to be an unnecessary burden handed down to us by our Puritan-Victorian ancestors. As a result, it happens rarely that a person feels his own guilt consciously as a pressing problem.

Far be it from me to trouble a blissful state of innocence! If the reasoning of easy-going Christianity or the psychology of moral nihilism were working I'd be most content to let the matter drop. But the fact is that our guilt has not been resolved, only repressed, and we do continue to bear our guilt as an inner burden. This does not improve anything. Leaving the problem unconscious prevents us from reaching a solution, for we cannot experience forgiveness until we know what we feel guilty about. If we do not face our guilt consciously we are likely to find it transposed into a psychosomatic illness (as with the man sick of the palsy, Luke 5:18 ff.), or find ourselves prone to accidents, or suffer from nameless anxieties, or defeat ourselves constantly, or be afraid to die, or endure any one of countless other kinds of pointless pains. While there is such a thing as a "guilt complex" which should be dealt with psychologically, there is also a genuine personal guilt which is an inevitable and necessary part of being alive.

We might glance for a moment at the errors in certain psychological and easy-going Christian solutions. The Freudian approach says substantially that guilt springs from the superego. The superego is described as a judgment mechanism built into the mind, as the accumulated result of parental, religious, and social instruction in right and wrong. Freudians feel that the superego is responsible for guilt, and particularly that its moral judgment collides with the natural cravings and instincts. While they are willing to grant that we need a certain amount of superego in order to keep an orderly society, still, in general, the goal of Freudian therapy is to ease tension and anxiety by reducing the amount of superego and hence making it easier for the individual to fulfill his pleasure-seeking natural cravings, particularly the sexual ones.

There is as a matter of fact some truth in this analysis of guilt, for what we feel guilty over is often conditioned by our social views, and this often tortures and misguides our

[*51*]

conscience. To a certain extent therapy will always consist in the re-education of conscience so that we can accept our natural human self. The Puritan conscience with its strong prohibitions against bodily desires is a case in point, and we are all grateful to Sigmund Freud for pointing this out. Of course the development of a heightened conscience was an important weapon in the hands of the ego in the struggle against the chaotic forces of nature. We would, after all, be pretty sorry human beings if we were only like animals, satisfying momentarily any bodily lust or craving. But having learned the lesson that our ego must be strong enough to face our desires, the Freudians are right in claiming that it is time we learned to accept some of our cravings as natural and desirable.

Jung does not speak of the superego as such, but he does speak of "collective thinking," by which he means generally held opinions which can take possession of our mind, though they are not really our own and often even conflict with our own truth. The superego reflects the collective morality of our group, but is only part of the larger area of collective thinking which throttles our true creativity, because it does not spring from our own individuality or from God but from prevailing opinion.

Some psychologists of the Freudian school fail to see that there is a source of morality which originates neither from instinctual conscience nor from built-in morality of parents and society, but from God in the sense of our own higher self, and which requires from us a morality which consists of following our own inner truth. Some things are wrong, not because society says so, but because they contradict our deepest and truest nature. For instance, abortion may be regarded by the unconscious of a woman as a sin, not because the law says it is illegal but because it is against her own nature. Religious morality, such as the Ten Commandments, is a projection or externalization of our own inner truth (or voice of God). Moral commandments have validity, not because they are absolutely right in themselves, but because they are generalizations of what the voice of God within tells every man about his own life. It is a most important step when we no longer depend upon the maxims of Church and society for moral guidance but are directly guided by our own inner truth. And let us not make any mistake about it: the law of the soul is every bit as demanding as the law of men.

A woman consulted me because of her depressions and psychogenic symptoms, which, her doctor said, were not physical in origin. At one time she had engaged in certain sexual practices (highly irregular means of achieving mutual orgasm with a man to whom she was not married), and she had reassured herself that times had changed, and God didn't really hold people guilty any more for such things. This way she had only rationalized her guilt and made it unconscious. However, in the course of following her dreams there were repeated and unmistakable allusions to these experiences. Inwardly she simply would not accept them; one might say that her soul was trying to vomit them up. Only when she accepted her guilt, realized her remorse and confided her experiences to the counselor whom she trusted did she become relieved from the unconscious bondage to her unacceptable memories. The conscious personality of the dreamer had, in modern fashion, accepted the sexual episodes as all right. She just wondered why she kept getting sick. It was her dreams which revealed to her that her unconscious refused to tolerate what had happened and so tried to force her to deal with herself.

Sigmund Freud has shown us that we cannot repress our

sexual nature in the name of religion. But neither can we repress our religious and moral nature in the name of instinct. There is a balance to be struck between the two. All one-sided repression has disastrous consequences. This is the reason why some psychological theories cannot solve the problem of guilt. There are times when it is necessary to feel guilty, because only through feeling guilty can we be restored.

I wonder how many times the following true story has repeated itself. A woman consults with a psychiatrist and admits her guilt over an adulterous affair. She had previously consulted with another doctor who told her that she was simply following her instinct and should not feel guilty. But since the guilt was persisting the second doctor sent her to a clergyman, to whom she repeated her story and revealed her guilt. However, the clergyman also failed, because he calmed her with the reassurance that we all make mistakes sometimes, and that God forgives us. No doubt he thought to be kind, understanding and forgiving, but in actuality he was being cruel. The woman returned to her psychiatrist, and it was he who had to turn priest and eventually help her to really feel God's forgiveness.

The dragon is two-headed. Mostly we do not take either our guilt or the possibility of being forgiven seriously enough. In spite of thinking "it doesn't matter," when we are at last confronted with our guilt we feel despair, and think that we never can be cleansed. This seems like a contradiction, for one would suppose that having rationalized away our guilt we would find it easy to accept forgiveness, but oddly enough it is just the rationalist who falls into despair when finally confronted with his guilt.

So it is not surprising that this problem always reappears in our dreams. Sometimes they remind us of our forgotten guiltiness, at other times they tell us restoration is possible. Our dreams always are trying to compensate the one-sided conscious attitude of "my guilt doesn't matter," or the despairing attitude "there is no hope for me."

Let us draw some conclusions:

1. We have looked in this chapter at further dreams, and I have given the reader the interpretations arrived at by the person seeking counsel and myself. Dreams, of course, cannot be put into test tubes and made the subject of experiments like other empirical facts. Whether or not an interpretation is true can be judged only by the extent to which the dreamer feels it to be meaningful, by comparison with other dream material from the interpreter's experience, and above all by the subsequent course of events. Again we come to the same conclusion as we did in the first chapter, that there lives within us what seems like an unconscious source of wisdom which helps us to see ourselves in a different perspective from what we had before and which seems to work toward the healing and wholeness of the personality. This wisdom uses dreams as communications, and it enables us to understand consciously these symbolic messages. I have used the word "wisdom" to describe the reality behind our dreams. From time to time in other places in this book I may refer to the "purposiveness" of our dreams, or even the "intelligence" behind our dreams. Using these terms personifies the unconscious as though it had a distinct will like our conscious mind. Strictly speaking, this is scientifically unjustified, since we simply do not know what the unconscious is in itself, even though we speak of it as though it were a single psychic entity. I use these terms because the unconscious does indeed impress me personally as having purpose and wisdom. I feel as Jung did when he wrote regarding amazing dreams which came to

him as a child, "Who was it speaking in me? Whose mind had devised them? What kind of superior intelligence was at work?" [3]

2. Dreams speak to us through symbols. All over the world, and all throughout history, men have always been dreaming. There are of course many different languages, but in the dream we have a universal language which "thinks" and expresses itself through symbols. This archaic language transcends all conscious verbal language barriers. Its symbols originate from two sources. One source is the individual's personal experience. Thus the little dog was the dreamer's very own dog. But there are other symbols which we cannot understand unless we descend to another source common to all men. By understanding what the earth, whiteness, and the square have meant to men throughout the centuries we found the meaning of these symbols of the dream. So we touched upon what Jung calls the "Collective Unconscious," and we could glimpse into the universal substratum of psychic life with its potentialities of development.

3. If we recognize the apparent purpose behind the dream, the deep source it draws upon for its symbolic material, and its compensatory function in the service of psychic balance, then we must ask the question, what are dreams driving at? And the possibility emerges that they are connected with an unseen goal of the personality which does not originate from the conscious ego but from some unknown, unconscious source. What might this goal be? The symbols of the circle, the round table, and the square, which we have encountered in our dream studies thus far, suggest that this goal may be described as wholeness of personality, or as emergency of a psychic totality in which all qualities of the personality are contained.

[56]

4. Margaret's dreams, which were of great personal help to her, dealt with a spiritual problem which is shared by most people today. The whole area of guilt (What is guilt? How does one find release and forgiveness?) is a problem most men do not face consciously, but wrestle with unconsciously. The Church continues, of course, to hold up to men the symbol of the Cross, and therefore it must proclaim God's eternal forgiveness. But forgiveness is a work of the soul, and unless the Church's message becomes engaged in that which is really happening within people it cannot hope to be very effective. Dreams such as Margaret's suggest that the Church would do well to dogmatize less about the nature of ultimate reality and listen more carefully to the soul of man through which our dreams speak to us.

III

Things Visible and Invisible

"And he was transfigured before them, and his face shone like the sun, and his garments became white as light."[1]

So far we have dealt with dreams concerned with specific psychological-religious problems. In this chapter we will look at a different kind of dream experience. The first example is a dream of my father's a week before he died.

My father, like myself, was an Episcopalian priest, as was his own father and grandfather. But he had entered the priesthood late after a period of turbulent years. As a young man he learned engineering drafting in various New England machine shops, and then went to college relatively late in his life. After graduation he taught Latin for a short time, and finally, motivated by boredom, so he told me, he went to China, where he worked as a teacher and engineer of sorts, and as a lay missionary.

I have always guessed that his delayed entry into the ministry was due to conflicts with his own father—their relationship apparently was quite ambiguous—but eventually while still in China, and at the age of about thirty-two, he was ordained to the Episcopal ministry. At about this time he married my mother, herself the daughter of Presbyterian missionaries in China. After a short time together in China, they returned to the United States, where my father took a parish in New Jersey. Here he was the rector for twenty-three successful years. When he became older he resigned to take a less exacting church in Massachusetts and eventually made his home in Westboro outside of Worcester.

Although my father had no special knowledge or training in modern psychology, he was a born pastor, and his relationships with his parishioners were fruitful. You might say he was an excellent example of a kind and wise Yankee minister, one of the unsung heroes of the Church who in spite of personal inner conflicts have ministered to anxious souls throughout the ages. Much of his pastoral experience he recorded in his book, *God's Healing Power*,[2] written shortly before his death. During his lifetime I never knew him to record or be aware of a single dream. And even when I, his son and fellow priest, became intrigued by dreams he remained unaffected.

About eight years before he died there came the first sign of angina pectoris, which became gradually worse and increasingly limited his activity. During the last two years this was also accompanied by a failing kidney. Consequently, there were many trips to the hospital; these trips were painful, humiliating, and depressing. Priest or not, every one of us is also just a man, and during one of these bitter illnesses he told me of his own anxiety over death, which he knew could not be far off. Then, one week before he died, he dreamed the following dream. He sensed its meaning immediately and told it to my mother, who recorded it. These are her words:

In the dream he awakened in his living room. But then the room changed and he was back in his room in the old house in Vermont as a child. Again the room changed: to Connecticut (where he had his first job), to China, to Pennsylvania (where he often visited), to New Jersey, and then back to the living room. In each scene after China, I [my mother] was present, in each instance being of a different age in accordance with the time represented. Finally he sees himself lying on the couch back in the living room. I am descending the stairs and the doctor is in the room. The doctor says, "Oh, he's gone." Then, as the others fade in the dream, he sees the clock on the mantelpiece; the hands have been moving, but now they stop; as they stop, a window opens behind the mantelpiece clock and a bright light shines through. The opening widens into a door and the light becomes a brilliant path. He walks out on the path of light and disappears.

My father knew of course that this was a dream of his approaching death, but no longer did he have any anxiety. When he died a week later it was in complete peace; he fell asleep at home and "forgot" to awaken. We had a special stone marker made for his grave—it has etched into it the "path of light" down which he went.

It is not uncommon for people to dream of their death. While I do not have enough of such dreams to draw any definite conclusions, yet it is my impression that some show the coming event as a great calamity and some as something beautiful. Perhaps this depends upon how well prepared we are for it, and to what extent we have lived a full life. Certainly in this dream the allusion to death is unmistakable. The stopping of the hands of the clock shows that time had ended for my father, and the actual occurrence of death soon after bears this out. By the series of flashbacks through the different stages of his life, the dream seems to gather up his life into a whole and represent the idea of the completely lived life. But the startling thing of course was the path of light which opened behind the clock and along which my father saw himself walk. The implication is obvious: that this was not the end, but the beginning of something else—that a new world had opened for him, beyond space and time.

Everyone's reaction to such a dream will be ambiguous. Our materialistic, rational side will rebel at the thought that reality can also extend beyond the grasp of our physical senses. Certainly every practical, down-to-earth man today would be greatly tempted to disregard such a dream, to say that it is mere foolishness. But the fact remains that the dream did happen. It was an actual event which took place, and therefore is worthy of careful consideration. "Nonsense," some will declare. "Unscientific." But *they* are the ones who are being unscientific, for they have made an unscientific assumption that all reality can be reduced to rationalistic, materialistic terms. Starting with this assumption they are bound to reject as unscientific any evidence that there is another dimension of reality. But the true scientist does not begin with assumptions but with the facts on hand; dreams are as much facts of life as anything else, only they cannot be grasped with hands or easily made into objects of scientific experiments.

Dreams such as this one hit the very core of our materialistic point of view. Everyone, of course, accepts the reality of this present, tangible, physical world; it is so obvious and is susceptible to experimentation and the scientific process. But the idea of a dimension of reality beyond space and time is counter to the collective thinking of our age. Indeed, communism officially repudiates this realm; and the Western world, while retaining the vestiges of religion, lives very much as though it also repudiated such a possibility.

Yet if a man is truly a Christian, he is pledged to take the invisible world seriously. In his creed (Nicene) he affirms his belief in "one God, the Father Almighty, Maker of heaven and earth. And of all things visible and invisible." In his sacraments he affirms his faith in an "inward and spiritual grace" of which the externals of the sacraments are the "outward and visible" signs. In his Bible he will find (as we will see later) on almost every page descriptions of an invisible, spiritual dimension of reality. The life of Jesus begins with dreams and angels, his ministry is ushered in with his baptism by the Spirit and temptation by the devil, it is climaxed by a transfiguration, and reaches its goal in a mystery, the Cross. Likewise in St. Paul we find an invisible world proclaimed which overpowers him on the road to Damascus and reveals itself by visions of being caught up into heaven, continuing with his allusions to "the principalities and powers of this world," his references to being "in Christ," to rebirth through the Cross, and so forth.

I am not trying to "prove" the reality of a spiritual world by referring to the Bible. If, of course, someone accepts the Bible as beyond doubt or criticism then the point is proved. Although I am personally deeply impressed by the Bible, I do not anticipate that many readers accept the Bible in this way; therefore I am not trying to build my point on "proof texts." But I am showing that the Christian religion was founded by men who believed in invisible reality and were ready to die for it. Other religions likewise share this conviction.

I want to go on now to two more dreams which are explainable only on the hypothesis that the dream source in the psyche is not limited by space and time. But first let me add a note of explanation. In offering the reader these particular dream examples I have been very selective. Many, many people have told me stories of dreams or similar experiences which seemed to have a foresight into the future or a knowledge of events taking place which consciousness could not possibly have recognized. There have been many such stories, particularly during World War II. However, I am presenting only examples from persons known to me, whose stability and character I can personally vouch for. The reach of dreams beyond space and time is not a subject matter for metaphysical and irresponsible speculation, but for careful and scientific observation. The best and most reliable dream source is always subjective, and up until now, no laboratory experiment has been conceived which could place such a study on the same footing as other natural sciences. I am well aware of all these difficulties, and abhor the dabbling in this field by undisciplined minds. Nevertheless, it is a fact that such dreams exist. They occur too regularly to stable personalities for us to close our eyes to them. As facts of life they demand consideration.

The following example comes from a middle-aged woman, well-known to me, of capable and honest intellect, and stable personality. She was not, by the way, used to recording or noting her dreams, and had no knowledge of their psychological importance. I record her experience in her own words:

> This dream occurred on December nine, nineteen hundred and forty-four. Our baby had died suddenly on November twenty-ninth, nineteen hundred and forty two, at the age of four months. In my dream (I was asleep) I saw a young woman of about thirty grasping the hand of a small boy, just learning to walk. I knew instantly that the boy was ours although both figures faced away from me. I noticed his sturdy little legs particularly. They were running freely and happily up a gentle slope of greensward dotted with flowers—the color of these latter were indescribable—they were not of this world.

[63]

The young woman wore a loose dress of indeterminate color, with a girdle at the waist. I felt very close to her. I thought that she was someone very near to me.

I awakened my husband to tell him of my dream because it was so vivid, and I got such great comfort from it. I said, "I believe that was my grandmother with our baby, because I felt so close to her and he is all right because she is taking care of him." I felt very happy. My husband noted the time —one-thirty A.M.

The next morning I received a telegram that my mother had died at one-thirty A.M. Having had that dream, I went through the funeral with never a thought of grief. I have never grieved for my mother or baby since.

Let us avoid a tendency to metaphysical explanations of the dream symbols. We simply do not know how to interpret the symbols of the hill, the flowers and the age of the little boy in the dream. They point to the continuance of life in another reality, but beyond that we can say little. But we can point to two indisputable facts: first, that the dream occurred at the same time as the death of the dreamer's mother; second, that it brought an irrational but profound reassurance. The first fact demonstrates that the unconscious source of our dreams is not necessarily limited by space and time as is our conscious mind. The second fact manifests that real religion is not based, as some would have it, on fabrications of man's conscious mind, or a desire to prolong a childish dependence on parental figures, but upon our innate recognition that our space-time reality is affected by another kind of reality, that the worlds "visible and invisible" of the Nicene Creed actually exist.

Now for the next example. Here the dreamer herself is unknown to me, and I am relying upon a friend who recorded the dream and later gave it to me. He is very trustworthy and knew the dreamer quite well. This dream is so striking and so typical that it is well worth recording here in the words of my friend:

> The dreamer dreamed three nights in succession of seeing a pool of dark water with leaves floating in it, and under the leaves a body. On the third day she was working in her kitchen and with no reason at all, she ran across three front yards into a neighbor's yard, and there it was: an abandoned fish pond and in it a body, floating under dead leaves. It was the body of her small son! Thanks to the dream which her inner being understood even though her outer consciousness did not, she reached him in time and he was saved by artificial respiration and suffered no harm. Had she not been warned by God in a dream, her son would have drowned. On the other hand, if she had known someone who could have helped her interpret the dream, she could have seen to it that the pond was protected by barbed wire or in some other way and her son would not have fallen into it at all.

Like our other example, this dream shows how the unconscious dream source can "know" of events inaccessible to our conscious minds, limited as they are by space and time. That there could be a reality beyond space and time, and that the psyche is capable of contacting it, is an hypothesis strange and foreign to our whole materialistic outlook.[3] Science itself has discovered so much that is remarkable in the universe that the scientifically minded person must take seriously Hamlet's warning, "There are more things in heaven and earth, Horatio, Than are dreamt of in your philosophy."

But if we are willing to look upon such dreams as natural facts, then the ultimate source of man's religious instincts appears to be from a deeper kind of reality than anything so far conceived by our conscious minds. The source of our

[65]

religion is far deeper than either the superficial theories of many psychological schools or the lamentable intellectualism of many of our contemporary theologians.

We must not naïvely suppose, however, that such dreams as these allow us to sink back complacently into conventional religious attitudes. To the contrary, they raise almost as many snakes as they kill, as the saying goes. Strange questions are prompted by a dream such as the above: why does this mother receive this dream, and not another mother? Why should her child be saved but another child the same day be drowned? On what basis does "God" make this selection? And what kind of a God is it who works through such a natural event as the dream? It would seem if we take our dreams seriously, then our nice, neat, dogmatic theories about God no longer suffice. "God" becomes an unknown reality to be explored; we are overwhelmed by our lack of knowledge and understanding, and the intellect, hitherto our favorite means for deluding ourselves that we know something, no longer seems like an effective weapon in the face of such apparently irrational realities. Small wonder academic theologians have preferred to ignore their nightly dreams: the Voice of God can be extremely disturbing!

I want to add an emphatic note of warning. I have included this chapter on the connection of dreams with a reality beyond space and time because it is important for our proper scientific and religious understanding, and I have emphasized that such dreams do occur with enough frequency that we must regard them as undeniable facts. But the reader should not suppose that he will find such dreams occurring to himself very often, if at all. Such dreams which anticipate the future are extremely rare and seem to occur only under special kinds of situations, particularly in highly emotional or archetypal (typical) life situations, or in cases of extreme urgency or overwhelming danger when it is a matter of life and death. For this reason they are especially numerous in time of war. But in the ordinary course of life they are simply not met with, and the vast number of our dreams are concerned with things more close at hand.

Let us now briefly summarize our findings:

1. Some dreams, occurring unpredictably but with surprising frequency at the critical moments of life, are explainable only on the hypothesis that they are based on a reality beyond space and time. This fact suggests that man's religious instincts may be partly founded upon an unconscious perception of an invisible reality which underlies his conscious existence. As St. Paul puts it, "For now we see through a glass, darkly; but then face to face." [4]

2. The dreams of this chapter illustrate once more the extreme autonomy of the unconscious psyche. Truly our conscious thoughts are not the only inhabitants of the house! We share our living quarters with another kind of psychic reality, which we call the unconscious because ordinarily it is unconscious to us. It is this unconscious source of our dreams which compensates our conscious viewpoints, by bringing us communications and realizations which consciousness by itself cannot possibly know.

3. Yet for all we know of the unconscious and the nature of the dream, its workings remain essentially "irrational," which means our dreams are not reducible to any rational or logical system of thinking. Like the wind, which, speaking in Jesus' poetical words, "blows where it wills, and you hear the sound of it, but you do not know whence it comes or whither it goes," [5] so our dreams have a seemingly capricious, irrational, but highly meaningful character.

[67]

4. It is this highly meaningful character of our dreams that makes us consider whether they come from some kind of purposive striving within us that is superior to our conscious aims. Men have always called an experience with such an extrahuman purpose in life an experience with "God," as we will see in our chapter on the Bible. Submitting our human consciousness to nightly scrutiny from the "unseen commentator of our soul" is an exciting, rewarding, healing, but sometimes frightening experience. It makes a mockery of much of our intellectualized theology or superficial, materialistic scientism.

IV

Nicodemus Today

"Jesus answered and said unto him . . . Except a man be born again, he cannot see the Kingdom of God. Nicodemus saith unto him, How can a man be born when he is old? can he enter the second time into his mother's womb, and be born? Jesus answered, Verily, verily, I say unto thee, Except a man be born of water and of the Spirit, he cannot enter into the Kingdom of God." [1]

If dreams are as important as I have indicated, then why should there be such ignorance about them today? Why are people so deaf to the voice which comes to them in their sleep, and why are there so many misconceptions about the meaning of the dream experience? We do not hear about them in our seminaries, or from our Christian pulpits, or from our doctor. The reason cannot be laid to ignorance. The Christian has his Bible, which as we shall see tells him clearly of the importance of the dream. And we all have had fifty years to read Freud and Jung, who have spoken to us in a modern way about dreams.

One of the many reasons why we close ourselves to the message of our dreams is fear. It is frightening to think that our dreams have meaning, for they might compel us to consider all kinds of unpleasant or surprising facts about ourselves. An encounter with the unconscious can be an agonizing, relentless dialogue, which we may often wish to avoid. But another reason, which we will discuss at length in this chapter, is that "Nicodemus" is still alive today in the thinking of modern men.

Poor Nicodemus! He had gone to Jesus because he had heard about the renowned teacher, and instead of something he could understand, Jesus only talked to him about being "born again." Jesus of course was speaking symbolically, not in order to deliberately obscure things, but because this is the only way the reality of unseen things can be conveyed. But Nicodemus was too encased in his literal, material point of view to understand. He could only say, "Can he enter the second time into his mother's womb?"

It is this literal, materialistic, preconceived kind of thinking which Nicodemus represents that blocks us from the messages of our dreams. With Nicodemus' attitude possessing us, we will not understand the dream's spiritual aspect. But unfortunately his thinking is typical for our age.

This Nicodemuslike point of view which blocks us from our dreams is what we can call "collective" or "mass" thinking. It appears whenever our minds and hearts are not our own, but are conditioned by generally prevailing opinions.[2] Collective thinking consists of all those attitudes and prejudices which we acquire from our parents, compatriots, teachers, and our present overly intellectual and material culture. It throttles our individuality and prevents us from hearing the creative voice within. Its extent and effects are far more subtle and prevalent than we realize, for from the time of our birth we have breathed it in, like a subtle poison in the air.

Collective thinking persistently influences our ideas and philosophies. But it also affects everything we say or do, and our entire life and being. It may come from the preacher in the pulpit whose ideas are not his own but belong to the invisible host of his supposed spiritual authorities. But it may equally well exist in the woman who keeps her house and lives her relationships, not in accordance with her true feelings, but as though the opinions of her mother were standing by whispering to her what to do. Our possession by collective thinking results in both psychological conflicts and spiritual sicknesses. I could cite instances where specific clinical symptoms, such as acute depression, or possession by compulsive ideas such as that of having a cancer were caused primarily by collective thinking which possessed the individual. In these cases, the source of the specific psychological symptoms is not to be found in past trauma, but in the present inhibition of the individual's creative urge. Looked at more broadly, the possession of our whole culture by collective attitudes is better described as a spiritual sickness. For us it has taken the shape of dictatorial systems involving us in spiritual struggle against them.

Nowhere is collective thinking more conspicuous than in the way it causes us to ignore, or distort, the meaning of our dreams. In the case of the Church, dreams are not considered at all. During my years of training to be a priest there was not one single word spoken to me about the dream. In Biblical commentaries, there is scarcely a thought given to the significance of the dream to religious experience, and this in spite of the great number of dreams in the Bible, and the high regard in which they were held by the early Church. And as for preaching on a dream from the pulpit, it is virtually unheard of. But the situation is equally bad in secular disciplines, where dreams, though not so completely ignored, are misunderstood and distorted by the preconceived viewpoint of collective thinking.

Consider this following example; I select it because it represents a typical, but not the worst, of the prevailing attitudes toward the dream. In the section entitled "That's a Good Question," on page 18 of the June, 1960, issue of the magazine *Today's Health*, a medical doctor answers the following question:

I have a dream from time to time in which a ferocious lion is chasing me. It hasn't caught me yet, but I usually wake up with my legs aching from having run so hard. What do you suppose is the cause?

The doctor gives this answer:

In general, there are two types of dreams. One is caused by influences to which the dreamer has been exposed, usually during the preceding day, although on occasion considerably earlier influences may suddenly produce a dream. The other type is what might be called spur-of-the-moment dreaming. In this virtually anything may be responsible, such as some strange noise that is not enough to waken one but is noted by the subconscious mind. With incredible rapidity, the mind constructs a situation to fit the noise or other disturbing influence. It is amazing what intricate details may be "thought up" in this way even by persons who are not ordinarily very imaginative.

In your case, there is a rather strong suggestion that the chase sequence is due to pain in your legs. Your mind, recognizing this pain, has you chased to explain it. It would be a good idea to have studies made by your physician, to determine whether there is some physical cause of the pain. If there were no pain, you might still have this type of dream because of some frightening earlier experience, the lion representing perhaps an individual of whom you are afraid. The subconscious mind often uses symbols in reliving disturbing experiences.

Notice what the doctor tries to do. First, if possible, the psychic event of the dream will be reduced to a physical stimulus; that is, the whole thing is due to a pain in the leg. This facile answer is passed off without explanation and with glib authority. What possible scientific basis there could be for such a statement is difficult to imagine; it is in fact not a scientific statement at all but a collective opinion. Second (just in case no physical ailment turns up) is the resort to the most mundane possible psychological explanation. In this case the lion does not any longer equal the pain in the leg but "someone whom you fear." Third is an explanation from external stimuli: the dream might be due to some strange noise not sufficient to awaken the dreamer but loud enough to affect the subconscious. We know dreams sometimes do include an external stimulus in their story, but this is rare, and even in such cases the dream uses the stimulus in its own way and for its own purpose. So these explanations all leave great questions staring us in the face. The doctor himself asks one without realizing it when he says naïvely, "It is amazing what intricate details may be 'thought up' in this way even by persons who are not ordinarily very imaginative." What about these "amazing intricate details" which occur even in "unimaginative" people? Do they have no meaning? This seems to be taken for granted here without further examination. Another question concerns the lion. Who is this lion? Why does the dream select a lion to pursue the dreamer? If "lion" equals physical pain, why dream about it? If the dreamer is afraid of a person, why not dream of the person instead of the lion? By remaining rooted in a concretistic interpretation the dream cannot be understood at all: What seems like a rational explanation explains nothing, and the whole dynamic nightly encounter which takes place between conscious and unconscious remains unrecognized.

For reasons which will appear in a later chapter, it is

[73]

perilous to try to analyze any dream without knowing the dreamer, the dreamer's circumstances at the time, and the dreamer's associations about the dream symbols. It is interesting, however, how often people do dream of lions, which often depict a devouring, instinctive aspect of the unconscious realm of the psyche. In this case the dream captures the same image as did St. Peter, who warns us, "Your adversary the devil prowls around like a roaring lion, seeking some one to devour." [3]

Quite probably the dream depicts the dreamer's relationship to her unconscious instinctuality. Because she rejects it, it takes on a devilish, devouring aspect. In what more pointed way could a conflict between conscious and unconscious be described than in this repeated dream of a lion chasing the dreamer? Such a dream would amount to an invitation for the dreamer to recognize her inner adversary. Similar, or possibly deeper, more symbolic meanings to the dream, depicting a vital relationship between ego and unconscious, have the door shut upon them because of a point of view which insists on reducing psychic things to concretistic terms.

So it is that we are possessed today by collective thinking, and this results in a serious spiritual sickness. But what do the dreams themselves say about this problem? Are they aware of the situation which exists in our conscious minds? To see this let us return to our friend Margaret. Margaret continued her counseling even after the first problem of forgiveness for her past misdeeds had been resolved. She is one of those people who are engaged upon an insatiable search for God and their own true self. But in the course of her counseling she seemed to have run into a block of some kind which prevented her from proceeding further, although no special psychological problem or unresolved human relationship seemed to be standing in her way. In this situation she had the following dream:

The dream began in an average-size room with a rectangular table, at which three or four people were seated, working with paper, letters and other clerical materials. It seemed to be near the close of the day, as things were being done in a rush in order to stack the loose papers according to size into orderly piles. During this rush we were discussing the subject of TB. Although I was among the group I didn't see myself. Suddenly Dr. X appeared in the doorway and came into the room. He appeared to be very angry and began to denounce me for having TB and not revealing it to the proper authorities. He said it was a terrible thing to do. He was very hostile and angry and looked at me with piercing eyes. I was afraid, but tried to explain that I had complied with the rules, and that a chest X-ray had been taken every year. I told him I had some old scars from pneumonia which I had many years ago, but that I was not aware anything was wrong.

The scene suddenly changed. Now the subject was not TB but a mishandled telephone call. The only person I saw or heard was Dr. X, who was still very angry at me over this particular telephone call in regard to TB, which I had presumably handled very badly. I tried to explain that I had not taken the call, but that I did know who did. Dr. X then asked me who the doctor was who had taken the call. I refused to give him the doctor's name, and Dr. X threatened he would find out for himself. But how would it help to give him the young doctor's name and involve another in my difficulty? I said, "I will leave, but we all know I am telling the truth and this alone is important to me."

The dreamer adds: "This dream was very vivid and more like a nightmare. I awakened with tears in my eyes, feeling unhappy. I was not excited but seemingly resigned to the

situation. Dr. X in the dream is not at all like this in real life.
I have never seen him angry. He always appears to be calm,
kind and gentlemanly. However, there was no mistake: it
was Dr. X."

This is a long dream which centers around a confrontation between the dreamer and an angry doctor who criti-
cizes her for ignoring her TB. The dreamer attempts to
defend herself, but the doctor is not to be moved. In the
second sequence, the doctor's anger is directed against a
"younger doctor" who does not appear directly in the
dream but is alluded to. The dreamer defends the young
doctor and insists that she is telling the truth. We have here
a good illustration of the *auseinandersetzung* (dialogue)
which takes place between conscious and unconscious. The
point of view of consciousness is expressed by the dreamer
herself; the point of view of the unconscious is taken by the
doctor.

Why should the doctor be considered the spokesman for
some of the dreamer's unconscious thoughts? In Chapter
VII, "The Nature and Structure of Dreams," I will talk
more completely about the meaning of male figures in the
dreams of a woman. For now we must content ourselves
with some essentials of feminine psychology. Women often
dream of women figures, who reflect different aspects of
themselves. We had occasion to discuss this kind of figure
in our chapter on the shadow. But we also find male figures
who play quite a different role. From our experience in
dealing with the feminine psyche we know that the feminine unconscious also contains certain masculine components. But the average woman will consciously identify
herself with her femininity; she remains unconscious of her
opposite polarity. The woman's unconscious masculine
characteristics are extremely important for her psychologi-

cal development, and they reveal themselves to her in her dreams, personified as a man. This masculine ingredient of her personality is termed by Jung "the animus." (One might suppose by this experience and reasoning that a man has within himself an unconscious set of feminine characteristics, and a correspondingly feminine dream figure. Such is the case, and she is termed by Jung "the anima.") In our dream the doctor is the dreamer's own unconscious "logos," or judge, who expresses a point of view within the unconscious part of her mind.

The point upon which Dr. X insists, in spite of the dreamer's denial, is that she has tuberculosis. What is the meaning of this tuberculosis? Since the dreamer did not actually have tuberculosis, the tuberculosis referred to must be symbolic of an inner or psychological sickness which is somewhat like TB. Consequently it must be an insidious disease, which does not betray its presence by conspicuous symptoms until it reaches a highly developed stage, relatively painless but deadly. Now the characteristics of tuberculosis as a disease of the body correspond exactly to the characteristics of mass thinking as a disease of the spirit. Tuberculosis attacks the lung, the area of breathing; mass thinking attacks the capacity for spiritual breathing (*pneuma*). In both cases the danger of being infected is great; both overpower us unnoticed. Tuberculosis can be diagnosed in good time only through exposing ourselves to X-rays; similarly mass thinking can only be recognized when we "X-ray" our own selves.

This dream wants to tell the dreamer that her realization of herself is in danger of being destroyed by mass thinking. The dreamer is so unaware of this condition that she objects strenuously (it is well known that the more valid an accusation is the more excited is our reaction), but it did

[77]

not escape the attention of her unconscious. Fortunately the creative centers of the unconscious are forever beyond such infections; these centers perceive the truth.

Why is Dr. X so very insistent, even angry, in this dream? We learn this in the second part, where a young doctor is accused of mishandling the telephone calls. Here I will confess to the reader that I recognized myself in the figure of the young doctor who was not receiving the phone calls correctly. Telephone calls are communications from a more or less distant source. I understood them as previous communications from the dreamer's unconscious which I, as the counselor, had not understood correctly and so had failed to pass on the message to the dreamer. My failure angered the dreamer's unconscious logos. In her loyalty she did not want to admit that she doubted my abilities, but in her dream these doubts did find expression. I went into all this with Margaret, and perhaps as a result of my increased awareness, her future dreams accepted my competence.

After this dream Margaret's development progressed well. The astonishing realization—"God is actually speaking to me!"—was no longer blocked.

From this helpful dream we can draw certain conclusions:

1. Our dreams are not limited to data from our personal life, but by a symbolic thinking relate us to issues in life beyond ourselves. In this case, the dream was not about sex, or persons the dreamer knew, or memories from the past, but about a hidden spiritual disease which has gripped our whole culture.

2. By taking into consideration our hitherto unconscious attitudes, we grow towards wholeness.

3. Where the ego and the unconscious move in separate

directions, a sort of enmity springs up between the two, as, for instance, in Tom's case. Clinically this results in a state of tension or anxiety. But the ego can learn to cooperate with the unconscious psyche in a process of creative growth and this process is shown in the dream. The essence of the process is an *auseinandersetzung* or dialogue between the ego and unconscious world within, through which the ego is brought ever closer to the psychic center. Jung saw in this process a striving to become one's true self and called it "individuation."

4. The dream shows us what seems like an unconscious source of wisdom. Clearly the unconscious psyche has access to a superior kind of knowledge. But notice also how important the ego is in the dream. Our psychological and religious growth depend equally upon our unconscious and our conscious mind. The unconscious sometimes possesses greater insight, but in the last analysis it all must go through the ego to be realized.

Inner growth is a walk. If we were to try and walk only with one leg we would make little progress; at best we might manage a wearisome hopping. Only if we step first with the right leg, then with the left, can we walk. Similarly we must draw upon both the conscious and the unconscious to get on spiritually and mentally. If we exclude our unconscious reality we become blocked and frustrated in our progress; if we include it we have an essential and helpful partner, but a partner with a will of his own.

Margaret's dream is unusually important because her problem is not unique to her but belongs to all of us. Like Nicodemus', our thinking is thoroughly conditioned by the literal, short-sighted attitudes of our time. The diagnosis the dream gives her of a spiritual tuberculosis is a diagnosis which belongs to us collectively, for, like Nicodemus, we

[79]

suffer from the inability to understand the life-giving symbolic language of the unconscious. But there is evidence in the Fourth Gospel that Nicodemus was cured of this incapacity, as also was Margaret. At least we are told in the 19th chapter of John's Gospel that Nicodemus had a hand in the risky business of burying Jesus after the Crucifixion, which suggests that Jesus' symbolically expressed message of spiritual reality found its mark at last. Through the same living voice of God we too can be released from collective opinions and attitudes, and breathe a life-giving spiritual air.

V

My Strength Is Made Perfect in Weakness

It is striking to observe the dreams of a person who is under analysis. The initial dreams may be concerned with one particular problem; but as soon as this is understood and acted upon they move on to others. It is like sitting at the foot of a brilliant teacher; when we have learned one lesson he moves on to the next one.

It is particularly interesting to watch this process because the dreams deal with many problems which the dreamer might never have realized existed or were important. Eventually, the dreams will succeed in bringing to the surface all the skeletons in the closet which the dreamer may not have faced. Past guilt feelings and traumatic experiences appear until they have been sufficiently understood and integrated by consciousness, thus losing their emotional force. But besides these unconscious personal contents the dreams will also include collective problems. There is no predictable order in the sequence of the dreams. The selection of dream material is beyond conscious control, and the conscious mind in following a series of dreams must be prepared to accept the lead of the unconscious.

This is not to minimize the importance of consciousness. There is a tendency in dream analysis to underrate the important role of consciousness and to do obeisance to the unconscious psyche. Actually both are of equal importance. The unconscious realm, having been in existence much longer than consciousness (the collective unconscious is as old as mankind, whereas the personal unconscious is only as old as the individual) naturally contains a greater store of wisdom, a knowledge superior to that which can be acquired in one lifetime. On the other hand, consciousness has the function of making decisions, of bearing pain and conflict, of understanding, examining and sorting the stuff of the personality. This is a demanding and sometimes frightening task. It is like a game of chess. Pawns and the other pieces are the unknown components of the personality, and the king is the ego. The king may seem relatively powerless, but without him there could be no game. A psychosis is in fact like a chess game without the king: the pieces are all there moving about, but the point of the game is lost. Thus, therapy for a psychotic demands the restoration of the ego: one has to put the king back on the chessboard.

The result of a series of dreams understood emotionally and intellectually and acted upon is the transformation of the personality, and the subordination of the ego to a greater psychic reality which manifests itself through the dreams. Sometimes people say: "But doesn't this preoccupation with yourself make you all the more egocentric?" It would if we were only preoccupied with our own ego, that is, with only our own personal, selfish desires. But someone who exposes himself to dream analysis subordinates his ego to a psychic principle of greater importance, and this can be baffling, painful, and humiliating. Egocentricity is reduced rather than increased, for we have to take second place to a greater psychic reality than that of our own ego.

Our dreams leave the uncanny impression that we are traveling down a road. Where does it lead? What is the goal of the dream process? We are not yet in a position to answer that question satisfactorily. It is a secret known only to the Creator. Somehow the whole meaning of life is involved. But we can at least give a partial answer. The dream process brings us closer and closer to the wholeness of the personality. But what might such a wholeness involve?

To understand what wholeness means we must first understand the extreme diversities within personality. We all contain potentialities for good and evil, light and darkness, love and hate; we possess masculine and feminine attributes, logos and eros; we are constituted of two psychic principles, consciousness and the unconscious. We share an instinctual nature with the beasts and a spiritual nature with the angels; we are thinking and feeling, perceivers of an outer and inner reality. Man is, as Jung puts it, a *complexio oppositorum*, a complexity of opposites. We are in fact so complex that our dreams contain a bewildering number of human and animal figures, all of them expressing different aspects or tendencies of personality.

As we outgrow childhood we identify ourselves consciously only with a minority of these tendencies. The rest, to which we deny expression, begin to war against the ego as if they wanted to force recognition. One might suppose in the face of this complexity of opposing tendencies that human personality would consist of fragments. In fact, this occasionally happens, as for instance in schizophrenia, when the crippled or destroyed ego is no longer capable of dealing with the opposing tendencies. Surprisingly this seldom happens; what protects us is the paradoxical unity of opposites within the personality.

There is something within the psyche which holds things together; like a magnet it draws the most varying things to itself, thus forming a center of personality where opposites are united. We may compare this center of personality to the nucleus of the atom, which holds flying electrons in orbit. Jung calls it the "self." It is at once center and circumference, and is that which includes the total person, conscious and unconscious. This self or psychic center cannot do the whole job by itself. It needs the ego to be, so to speak, the administrator of the personality. Without the ego's efforts the saving effects of the center could not become effective. But the ultimate resolution of psychic conflicts takes place in the center and not in the ego.

This center, or self,[1] is not an abstract idea. It is an hypothesis to account for definite and observable facts. The movement of the unconscious in the direction of wholeness can be adequately explained only by the concept of a psychic center which makes totality possible. Moreover this center is often represented in dreams by a symbol or image, which reveals the center's paradoxical nature. It is something that has always existed, is presently at work, and has yet to be born. It has always existed because the self is inherent in the psyche from the beginning; it is presently working because the self strives to effect an as yet unrealized wholeness; it is yet to be born because our wholeness must ultimately be recognized by consciousness and expressed through a consciously lived life. When all the diverse elements which constitute the total personality are sufficiently united to be embraced and expressed by our ego, then, figuratively speaking, the self is "born."

We have already seen some of the symbols of psychic wholeness in square and circle form. But this wholeness at which our dreams are aiming is a strange kind of wholeness. We will now look at some of its paradoxical qualities, with the help of a case history.

[*84*]

The dreamer in this case is a woman of considerable charm. Let's call her "Emily." Though of middle age, any man can see that she must have been a beauty as a girl. Her childhood had been unfortunate: divorced parents, much poverty, no cultural benefits, little education. This was especially unfortunate in her case because she had considerable native intelligence which had never been developed. She grew up without guidance and followed her feminine instincts without the benefit of counterbalancing principles. She became a night-club dancer, wandered for years from one night club to another, married early and unhappily and was divorced. A second marriage turned out better, but by this time things had gone too far; a severe drinking problem sprang up complicated by addiction to pills.

During these years she suffered from depression, confusion, and anxiety, with physical symptoms of simulated heart attacks and spells of dizziness. However, at the same time a religious feeling and determination to become well began to grow in her. This led her to join Alcoholics Anonymous and a little later a fundamentalist Protestant church, and with the help of these organizations she remained sober. Her attacks of anxiety, her times of confusion, and her strong desire for inner development led her to me.

In Emily's dreams two problems in particular emerged: (1) the need for her to accept herself as a person with natural instincts, and not to fear this side of herself, even though it had led her astray, and (2) her need to improve her thinking abilities. In fact, her attacks of confusion and dizziness proved to be caused by her lack of contact with her own thinking. Her intellectual abilities had dropped into the unconscious. In critical situations where they were specifically needed to help her orient herself she did not have them at her disposal and so she became dizzy. She made good progress, however, thanks to her love for truth and her courage. At the point where her self-acceptance and her ability to think independently began to grow she had the following short but impressive dream.

I have received a beautiful orchid; I desperately want to know who it is from.

Here we have a dream which is a model of seeming simplicity. There is virtually no action; there are no protagonists save the dreamer herself and the unknown bestower of the orchid. It is the orchid that claims the center of the stage; it arouses the dreamer's desire to know the giver. What shall we say of this orchid? Emily was first at a loss for any thoughts, yet eventually something did occur to her. The orchid is a treasured, beautiful flower which is not arranged in bouquets, but is admired by itself. It is often given by people as an expression of their devotion. It can be grown by men, but must be given special care in order to thrive. All conditions of growth must be just right; it is not enough to plant them and then leave them to themselves. In our climate their cultivation requires cooperation between man and nature. These associations give us the clue. The orchid represents those feelings which begin to flower in Emily as she approaches nearer to the center and the wholeness of her personality. It is of course only a step on the way and does not mean that her wholeness is accomplished. Still, it heralds the approach to the self, and to the capacity for feminine feeling which is in prospect for her like a beautiful present, as soon as she begins to grasp something of the perfection of the self.

It is interesting to compare the qualities of the orchid and the self. Both are individual and unique. Though all men share in certain respects the same self, yet it takes on unique, solitary form wherever it is consciously recognized. Further, the self, like the orchid, can be consciously cultivated. The fertile soil from which it grows is the unconscious; the gardener is consciousness. Finally, the harmony and integration of personality require the same cooperation between man and nature, consciousness and the unconscious, as does the cultivation of orchids. So it symbolizes on one hand the perfection of the center, on the other hand the flourishing of unique, individual feelings. But what kind of perfection is this perfection of the soul? There are two conceptions of what perfection involves. One concept is that perfection exists where there is no blemish, no stain of darkness. The traditional ecclesiastical concept of the perfect person is one free from sin, dark thoughts, or any contamination with evil. We might point to the Puritan ideal and Calvin's attempt to found the "City of God" in Geneva. But there is another concept of perfection also: it exists where things are whole, complete, in order and harmony as their Creator intended them to be. In this case, there might be darkness involved in the pattern, but it would be part of its order, functioning with the other elements in a harmonious way. We might better describe this perfection as "completeness."

In terms of personality, this kind of perfection or completeness would not involve the eradication of the natural man with his propensity toward instinctual behavior and passion, but rather the regrouping of the elements of personality into a whole. This "complete" man would have a harmonious relationship between all the opposite tendencies in himself, a feat which only God can accomplish. The contrast between perfection as lack of darkness, and perfection as completion, meaning the inclusion of darkness into a paradoxical whole, is a subtle, but vastly important, concept of psychotherapy.

What kind of wholeness do dreams describe? There can be no doubt that an image of perfection in the sense of completeness is contained in our unconscious center. The psyche does not contain any absolute goodness. To the contrary, our dark, natural side is a necessary part of the complete man. Man, like a gardener, can tend the inner process, but the final secret of his wholeness is known only to God. That, perhaps, is why Emily so "desperately" wants to know who sent her the beautiful orchid.

Of course such a dream does not mean that the goal is accomplished. Completion is always something we move toward. It is a reality we now approach closely, but then again move away from, as we follow our inevitable tendency to be unaware of ourselves. Nevertheless, the appearance of such a symbol in the dream may be taken as a sign of the increasing integration of the dreamer's personality.

To think of our wholeness as paradoxical completeness rather than perfection without blemish is hard for most of us. Emily also found it hard. Her instinctual nature had led her into so much trouble that she could not bring herself to accept it; she tried persistently to conform to a moralistic attitude toward life. "Christianity" and "nature" remained for her hostile opposites. In the midst of her struggle she dreamed the following dream:

> I was riding on a bus on my way to a large gathering, beautifully dressed. Upon arrival, in getting off the bus, I noticed to my consternation that I had a round hole in one of my stockings.

Here is a dream about which one might say: "What a strange dream I had last night. Just a lot of foolishness about a round hole in my stocking. It must have been what I ate for dinner." But as we have seen, dreams are not intentionally obscure; it is only our conscious understanding that is obscure. So it was with this dream.

Emily had several things to say about this dream. She connected her well-dressed appearance in the dream with her desire to appear "just right." She had thought herself attired beyond reproach; and now the hole!—it was most distressing.

The main feature of the dream is this neat, round hole in the stocking. She was unconscious of its existence until she got off the bus. The legs, being that part of our body which connects us with the ground, often stand for the "lower man," our instinctual desires and feelings. While attempting to appear just right, the dreamer actually is unconscious of the hole in her stocking. The natural, lower side of her nature is not yet sufficiently taken into account.

But what about this hole? We have already found dreams in which the circle appeared as a symbol of completeness, and recognized that through its form it seeks to express the mystery of wholeness. The round hole in her stocking expresses both an imperfection in her attire and the possibility of her completeness. It says, "If you would find your wholeness, you must not seek to appear perfect. Your wholeness wants to include also your imperfections. It is through these imperfections that you will recognize your wholeness as a human being. Perfection comes through imperfection." This is of course a tremendous paradox which defies rational explanation. But Christians should be used to thinking in terms of such paradoxes. St. Paul stated the same thing in the words which he heard from the Lord, "My strength is made perfect in weakness."

There is also another element to the dream, which is

significant; the bus from which the dreamer stepped. You will recall that as the dream began the dreamer was on the bus; she became aware of her true condition only when she stepped off it. Unfortunately, we do not have the dreamer's associations to the bus. It is always dangerous to risk too much interpretation when we do not have all of the dreamer's own ideas. Nevertheless, it is quite likely that the bus represented to her a public means of getting places, a collective service. Psychologically, this would mean: as long as the dreamer is contained in this public way of thinking she does not notice her true condition. Only when she steps off the bus, to walk on her own legs, that is to make her own efforts, does she realize what is her true condition. Only when we leave the collective way for our own individual way are we able to realize how paradoxical and unique wholeness is.

From these dreams we can again learn something:

1. They show us how the unconscious leads our attention not only to the past, but also to the future. The self within us guides us into our impending inner development; not only are we influenced by that which has gone before, but also by that which wants to become. To use a clumsy analogy: the acorn "knows" what the tree shall be. It contains within itself the "image" of the tree, and as the tree grows and unfolds from the acorn it grows and unfolds according to this image. The unconscious contains the image of the whole person we are to become, the "person in the mind of God." Our behavior is just as much determined by the attempts of the unconscious to realize this image in the course of our life as it is by what has happened to us in the past. Both are of equal importance.

2. The dreams teach us that wholeness may be a different matter from what we thought. It cannot be equated with mere social adjustment, for this would only mean a

total surrender to collective thinking, and this would be unbearable for the unconscious. To the contrary, like Christ, the whole person will necessarily come into opposition with society. Nor can it be equated with perfection in the sense of becoming a person without a shadow, without a negative thought or dark mood. Instead the dreams suggest an entirely new way of thinking about the whole man. He is a circle, including everything within him, a central point in which all is united, an orchid in which man's conscious mind and God's nature have cooperated to bring about something of exquisite beauty, a paradox par excellence whose very completeness involves his imperfection.

To work toward this wholeness is not an easy task. It involves a religious search for meaning as well as psychological insight, a lonely separation from the collective identity with other men, a painful looking into oneself and upon one's own shadow, the acceptance of a higher power within oneself to which one must submit. In the long run, the search for one's true self is a fascinating journey, with rich treasures, and great rewards. But it is a painful enterprise, and one which never ends. As we understand the depths of the opposites within us, and how torn and divided we are between the varying sides of ourselves which all make demands upon us, then it can be a frightening journey as well.

This is especially true in this Christian era when we have been so trained to accept only that which is "good" and to reject that which seems evil. This split between good and evil is universal today, and poses special problems to the world. More than with anything else, our dreams are concerned with this problem of opposites, and its resolution in a new and higher synthesis. For it is the central problem of our day; it touches the boundaries of our psychological knowledge and our spiritual insight.

[*91*]

PART TWO

Introduction

We have studied several dreams in the context of the lives of the dreamers. We began with some dreams about the relatively simple problem of the shadow. But the last chapter introduced a very subtle and paradoxical problem, the problem of the nature of wholeness. The following dreams will continue to deal with this problem. But we will digress now for a while to get more information about dreams before going on to the more difficult questions they raise.

So the next two chapters will deal more generally with dreams. The first one is about dreams in the Bible, and is written especially for those who wish to put dreams into a Christian perspective. The second chapter deals with the general nature and structure of the dream.

I wish I could also go into the dream material found in early Christian literature. This material in the writings of the Fathers is almost as impressive as that found in the Bible. Tertullian declared: "Almost the greater part of mankind derive their knowledge of God from dreams." However, this would take us beyond the scope of this book, and the interested reader must be content with the note following in which are listed a few of the many references to dreams and visions in early Christian literature.

The remaining chapters conclude our study of dreams, of the nature of the self and the peculiar problem it poses to the Christian. The final chapter defines more closely in what sense dreams are to be regarded as God's forgotten language.

NOTE

My collection of passages from the writings of the Fathers contains some 150 distinct references to dream material, including passages from all the major Fathers of the Church. To cite just a few of the most prominent:

Tertullian often cites dreams, wrote a psychological treatise on the soul which is surprisingly modern; it is here he stated that "almost the greater part of mankind derive their knowledge of God from dreams." (*De Anima* xliv.)

St. Augustine made careful note of many dreams. His Letters IX, CCXXVII, CLIX, his *Confessions,* and his *De Trinitate* II. 18, IV. 1, are especially important.

Origen equated both dreams and ESP phenomena with the activity of the divine Logos; see especially his *Contra Celsum* I. lxvi.

Cyprian, the great African bishop, looked to his dreams for practical guidance in making immediate decisions. (Letters IX, XXXIII, LXIII, LIII.)

Synesius of Cyrene wrote a detailed description of dreams in his *De Insomniis.*

Athanasius, champion of orthodoxy, asserted that in dreams the soul transcends the faculties of the body to hold divine communion with the angels. (*Against the Heathen,* par. 33.)

And of course we have an abundance of dream material in the legendary and apocryphal early Christian material, perhaps the most important of which is the *Shepherd of Hermas,* which is based entirely on dreams and visions. For a complete résumé of this, and later, material on dreams in Christian tradition, see the Reverend Morton T. Kelsey's excellent book, *Dreams: The Dark Speech of the Spirit.* Doubleday, 1968.

VI

Dreams and Visions in the Bible

To deal completely with the subject of the dreams and visions in the Bible would require a book in itself. For not only are there the passages referring specifically to dreams, but there are also passages referring to visions, appearances of angels, trances, and "being in the spirit," all of which are described in such a way that the distinction between them is not sharply drawn; the Bible regards dreams, visions, certain trances, appearances of angels, and experiences of the spirit in much the same way.

In regarding dreams and visions as similar in source, construction, and significance, the Bible is on solid scientific ground. All of us know from our firsthand experience what a dream is. Psychologically we call a dream an experience a person might have during sleep, i.e., during a naturally unconscious state. A dream is in fact a "story" which "happens" to us during sleep, of which we are a part, or at least a spectator. A vision can be understood as a "dream" we have while semiconscious or awake. If the unconscious breaks through into our consciousness during our waking state with a dreamlike image or action then we are experiencing a vision. It is sometimes supposed today that to have a dream is permissible enough, but to have a vision is a sign of insanity or mental derangement of some kind. This, however, is not the case. It is not the vision which is a sign of mental derangement, but the point of view from which the ego regards the vision. In insanity the vision is accepted as literal, external reality, and consciousness does not distinguish between the external and the internal world. In the normal ego, however, the vision is recognized for its subjective, internal nature. It is not the vision that is a sign of sickness, nor the unconscious that is "insane," but the ego which is sick or has lost its bearings, and the fact that the insane are more prone to visions than the more stable individual is simply due to the vulnerability of their weakened and shattered ego-structure to invasions from the unconscious.

When, therefore, the Book of Numbers says:[1] "And he said, 'Hear my words: If there is a prophet among you, I the Lord make myself known to him in a vision, I speak with him in a dream,'" thus equating clearly the common origin and significance of dreams and visions, it is resting upon very good psychological foundations. But the Bible likewise often equates the appearance of an angel with a dream or a vision. Take, for instance, the following passages from the Gospel of Matthew: As Joseph considers putting Mary away quietly after discovering her pregnancy we read that "the angel of the Lord appeared to him in a dream," bidding him to retain Mary as his wife and telling him her child is of the Holy Spirit.[2] Later, the Wise Men having found and worshiped the child Jesus are "warned in a dream not to return to Herod."[3] Immediately after, Joseph again is visited by an angel of the Lord in a dream, bidding him flee to Egypt for safety.[4] And after a sojourn in Egypt he is bidden once more by an angel in a dream to return to the land of Israel.[5] In still another dream the angel bids him to return not to Judea, but to Galilee.[6] We thus find in the first two chapters of Matthew no less than five dreams, and we further establish that every decision in this action-packed section is based upon a revelation

[99]

made by God through a dream.[7] Further, four of these specifically cite the appearance of an angel, so that the Bible clearly equates the revelations given by angels and the revelations by dreams and visions.

Matthew is not the only one who equates angels and dreams. We find, for instance, in Luke that Zechariah's experience with the angel Gabriel is a vision,[8] and that the angels who appeared to the women after the Resurrection were regarded as a vision.[9] To cite only one example from the abundant material in Acts: the Centurion Cornelius has an experience in which an angel comes to him in a vision.[10] And from the Book of Revelation we learn that the entire revelation given to John by an angel is a vision, a fact borne out by the visionary quality of the book as a whole.[11]

Even experiences "of the spirit" are frequently regarded by the Biblical writers as similar in kind to experiences of visions and dreams. The similarity between having a vision or dream and being "in the spirit" is abundantly shown, for instance, in the Book of Ezekiel, which we will have occasion to refer to later. Again and again in Ezekiel we read verses such as these: "He put forth the form of a hand, and took me by a lock of my head; and the Spirit lifted me up between earth and heaven, and brought me in visions of God to Jerusalem. . . ." [12] Ezekiel, however, is by no means the only book where experiences of the Spirit are equated with visionary experiences. St. Paul himself goes on to describe "visions and revelations of the Lord," [13] and the Book of Joel is quoted in the Book of Acts in this significant verse: "And in the last days it shall be, God declares, that I will pour out my Spirit upon all flesh, and your sons and your daughters shall prophesy, and your young men shall see visions, and your old men shall dream dreams. . . ." [14] We have then a very fine line indeed between visions, dreams, the appearance of angels, and an outpouring of the Spirit of God.

In the Book of Samuel, when Saul is not able to find God any longer, we read, "And when Saul inquired of the Lord, the Lord did not answer him, either by dreams, or by Urim, or by prophets." [15] Here we see dreams regarded along with revelations from the prophets (who themselves probably gained their knowledge through dreams), and with the sacred lots (Urim), as one of the three means by which a man might know the mind of God. In the story of the boy Samuel we read, "And the word of the Lord was rare in those days; there was no frequent vision." The story then goes on to describe Samuel's visionary experience with God whereby he ascertains the divine authority for his coming career.[16]

In I Chronicles the prophet Nathan receives the "word of the Lord" bidding him to speak to David regarding the house of the Lord. Later we read: "In accordance with all these words, and in accordance with all this vision, Nathan spoke to David." [17] Thus the source of the word of the Lord which came to Nathan was a vision. Further examples of the revelation of the divine will to men in a vision include the following:

"Of old thou didst speak in a vision to thy faithful one. . . ." [18]

"It was I [the Lord] who multiplied visions and through the prophets gave parables." [19]

And God spoke to Israel in visions of the night. . . . [20]

Now there was a disciple at Damascus named Ananias. The Lord said to him in a vision. . . . [He goes on to instruct him to heal Paul.] [21]

Peter receives the great vision revealing to him that all things are clean in the eyes of God. In verses 17 and 19 this is referred to as a vision.[22]

Paul is guided to go to Macedonia in a "vision . . . in the night." [23]

"And the Lord said to Paul one night in a vision. . . ." [24]

Since dreams and visions were regarded as revelations from God we would expect that abuses would enter into their interpretation. This condition we find to have been the case, when it is hinted at in Numbers, where dreams are referred to as the "dark speech" [25] of God. The prophet Jeremiah speaks quite clearly about the divine authorship of dreams, and he warns against false interpreters and those who pretend they have had dreams when they have not. For instance: "Do not listen to the words of the prophets who prophesy to you, filling you with vain hopes; they speak visions of their own minds, not from the mouth of the Lord." [26]

Is this reverence for dreams to be found everywhere in the Bible? Was it something peculiar to the Old Testament or the New? Was it late in the development of Israel or early? The divine authorship of the dream is found from first to last in the Bible! The Book of Genesis is filled with dream material, and the Bible closes with the Book of Revelation, which is itself entirely a vision. Turning to the Book of Genesis for a moment, we can summarize some astonishing and most beautiful dream material, beginning with an important manifestation of God to Abraham.

"As the sun was going down, a deep sleep fell on Abram; and lo, a dread and great darkness fell upon him. Then the Lord said to Abram, 'Know of a surety that your descendants will be sojourners in a land that is not theirs, and will be slaves there, and they will be oppressed for four hundred years. . . .' " Then after continuing with this prediction of things to come we read, "When the sun had gone down and it was dark, behold, a smoking fire pot and a flaming torch passed between these pieces. On that day the Lord made a covenant with Abram. . . ." [27] The Book of Genesis only hints at the epic dream experience which came to Abraham when he beheld God as a fiery furnace. We certainly have a precursor here of those experiences which have led men to picture the Holy Spirit as fire.

To appreciate the abundance of dream material in Genesis, consider only the following further examples: "But God came to Abimelech in a dream by night. . . ." [28] In this dream Abimelech is warned by God that Sarah is Abraham's wife.

> And Jacob went out from Beersheba, and went toward Haran. And he lighted upon a certain place, and tarried there all night, because the sun was set; and he took of the stones of that place, and put them for his pillows, and lay down in that place to sleep. And he dreamed, and behold a ladder set up on the earth, and the top of it reached to heaven: and behold the angels of God ascending and descending on it. . . . [29]

Joseph dreams of his sheaf standing upright in the field and those of his brothers bowing down, and then again, of the sun, moon and eleven stars bowing down to him. The seriousness with which this dream was regarded may be surmised by the hatred which it enkindled in his brethren, and the fact that "his father kept the saying in mind. . . ." [30] The chief baker and chief butler dream their dreams and take them so seriously that Joseph is called upon as an interpreter. Joseph says: "Do not interpretations belong to God? Tell them to me, I pray you. . . ." [31] Pharaoh dreams of the seven fat cows being devoured by the seven lean cows, and then again of the seven good ears of corn being swallowed up by seven withered ears of corn. When he asks Joseph to interpret them, Joseph says, "It is not in me; God will give Pharaoh a favorable answer." And later adds, "The dream of Pharaoh is one; God has revealed to Pharaoh what he is about to do. . . ." [32]

It is clear from these examples that in the Book of Genesis dreams were regarded as manifestations of divine intention, as one of God's ways of communicating with men. A person inspired by God might interpret dreams with great benefit to the dreamer, for through understanding his dreams and acting in accordance with them, Pharaoh was able to avert a great catastrophe.

There are entire books in the Bible which are asserted to be dreams or visions. The authors of the books of Obadiah, Nahum and Habakuk, claim that their books contain visions. Now how much of these books actually is visionary and how much is of more conscious origin is hard to say. Certainly the authors felt it important to claim them as visions in order to strengthen their authority.

Two other books in the Bible are of considerable interest with regard to dreams and visions: the Books of Job and Ezekiel. In the Book of Job we find that the one thing which Job, his three "friends" Eliphaz, Bildad, and Zophar, and his later antagonist Elihu, can agree upon is the significance of dreams. Eliphaz cites a vision as the source of his knowledge:

> "Now a word was brought to me stealthily,
> my ear received the whisper of it.
> Amid thoughts from visions of the night,
> when deep sleep falls on men,
> dread came upon me, and trembling,

which made all my bones shake.
A spirit glided past my face;
   the hair of my flesh stood up.
It stood still,
   but I could not discern its appearance.
A form was before my eyes;
   there was silence, then I heard a voice:
'Can mortal man be righteous before God?
   Can a man be pure before his Maker?' " [33]

We might note that the message Eliphaz received from this experience is a good and sound message. Eliphaz' error in argument was his conclusion that Job's misfortune was the result of great deliberate sin and that the remedy would be repentence, thereby missing the point of Job's human demand for justice.

Not only Eliphaz but Elihu as well regarded dreams as revelations from God, intended to sway us from our one-sided path in life, avert approaching catastrophe, and preserve our soul. He says:

"Behold, in this you are not right. I will answer you.
   God is greater than man.
Why do you contend against him,
   saying, 'He will answer none of my words'?
For God speaks in one way,
   and in two, though man does not perceive it.
In a dream, in a vision of the night,
   when deep sleep falls upon men,
   while they slumber on their beds,
then he opens the ears of men,
   and terrifies them with warnings,
that he may turn man aside from his deed,
   and cut off pride from man;
he keeps back his soul from the Pit,
   his life from perishing by the sword.' " [34]

[105]

And finally Job himself says:

> "Therefore I will not restrain my mouth;
> I will speak in the anguish of my spirit;
> I will complain in the bitterness of my soul.
> Am I the sea, or a sea monster,
> that thou settest a guard over me?
> When I say, 'My bed will comfort me,
> my couch will ease my complaint,'
> then thou dost scare me with dreams
> and terrify me with visions. . . ." [35]

The book of Ezekiel begins without any preparation (except the date) with these words, ". . . as I was among the exiles by the river Chebar, the heavens were opened, and I saw visions of God." [36] The prophet then goes on to a mighty vision which sets the tone of the entire book and completely dominates the next seven chapters. In fact, so mighty is this vision that there is frequently a reference back to this primary experience, even though other visions also haunt the prophet.

This basic vision of Ezekiel is especially interesting from a contemporary point of view because of its clear mandala symbolism. A mandala is a design usually found in Eastern religions. It depicts the idea of wholeness by a symmetrical shape or by a circular form. However, the Christian religion also knows mandalas, as for instance the so-called "rose windows" in many Gothic churches. These symbols well up from the depths of the psyche and express themselves autonomously in our dreams, visions, art, and religion.

In the case of Ezekiel's vision the mandala is contained in the image of the cherubim and of the whirling wheels. Notice in the description of the cherubim and emphasis upon the number four: there are four living creatures, each with four faces, one facing in each of the four directions.

These are terribly and wonderfully made creatures who seem to express by their quaternity something very important. We find that four in religious symbolism throughout the world has always stood for the number which embraces everything essential. There are four rivers that form the Garden of Eden, there are four corners that embrace all the earth, the heavenly Jerusalem will be laid out with four equidistant sides. Jung has shown that there are four functions of the psyche, which if they are all proportionately developed will lead a man to his own completeness.[37] The four is a number which stands for the All.[38]

We might also note, in passing, that the movement of the cherubim is described by Ezekiel in a manner which brings to mind the supposed movements of flying saucers. "And each went straight forward; wherever the spirit would go, they went, without turning as they went. . . . And the living creatures darted to and fro, like a flash of lightning." [39] This gives some credence to Jung's thesis [40] that the visions of flying saucers could be spontaneous projections from the unconscious with religious meaning.

Turning now to the fiery wheels, so well known from the Negro spiritual, "Ezekiel Saw the Wheels," we see again the compelling way in which the unconscious has seized the prophet. This time the image is in circular form. Like the cherubim, the wheels move in a strange way. The vision concludes with the sight of the remarkable God-man of fire, whom the Christian must take to be the pre-existent Christ and Jung would describe as the image of the self, that is, the wholeness of God as it has been realized in man.

Let us now range for a moment from the Book of Ezekiel to an Old Testament book of quite a different type, the Song of Solomon. This book is one which often baffles the Christian today, who cannot understand why a book of such sensuous quality should be included in the canon of the Old Testament. In fairness we must admit that this apparently baffled some of the ancients as well, who wrote many allegorical interpretations of the Song of Solomon attempting to translate its sensuously protrayed human love into an allegory of the love of God for Israel or Christ for His Church. The fact remains that the book consists of a collection of love songs and of poems portraying the love of man for maid in all its vividness and purity. Speaking from my own point of view, I cannot understand why we should find it so difficult to accept this beautiful book as religious in spirit. Is not human love one of the wonders of God? Is not beneath the yearning of man for woman and woman for man a yearning for wholeness, which is truly divine in origin?

Be that as it may, we have in the Song of Solomon two passages which almost certainly were originally dreams:

> Upon my bed at night
>> I sought him whom my soul loves;
> I sought him, but found him not;
>> I called him, but he gave no answer.
> "I will rise now and go about the city,
>> in the streets and in the squares;
> I will seek him whom my soul loves."
>> I sought him, but found him not.
> The watchmen found me,
>> as they went about in the city.
> "Have you seen him whom my soul loves?"
> Scarcely had I passed them,
>> when I found him whom my soul loves.
> I held him, and would not let him go
>> until I had brought him into my mother's house,
>> and into the chamber of her that conceived me.
> I adjure you, O daughters of Jerusalem,
>> by the gazelles or the hinds of the field,

that you stir not up nor awaken love
    until it please.[41]

I slept, but my heart was awake.
Hark! my beloved is knocking,
"Open to me, my sister, my love,
    my dove, my perfect one;
for my head is wet with dew,
    my locks with the drops of the night."
I had put off my garment,
    how could I put it on?
I had bathed my feet,
    how could I soil them?
My beloved put his hand to the latch,
    and my heart was thrilled within me.
I arose to open to my beloved,
    and my hands dripped with myrrh,
my fingers with liquid myrrh,
    upon the handles of the bolt.
I opened to my beloved,
    but my beloved had turned and gone.
My soul failed me when he spoke.
I sought him, but found him not;
    I called him, but he gave no answer,
The watchmen found me,
    as they went about in the city;
they beat me, they wounded me,
    they took away my mantle,
    those watchmen of the walls.
I adjure you, O daughters of Jerusalem,
    if you find my beloved,
that you tell him
    I am sick with love.[42]

In the first instance, the maiden on her bed at night seeks "him whom my soul loves." Not finding him, she goes out into the city at night, encounters the watchmen of the city, and ultimately finds her lover. Such an episode would scarcely have actually taken place in any young chaste Jewish maiden's life, but it could very easily have been a dream, and a dream fraught with deep psychological meaning if the lover whom the maiden seeks is the "inner man" or "animus" of whom Dr. Jung speaks. Our hypothesis that the source of this piece of poetry was actually a dream is borne out by the verses in chapter 5, where much the same plot is enacted (although this time the watchmen beat the maiden for wandering about alone at night), but which begins with these words: "I slept, but my heart was awake." In other words, the maiden was asleep, but her heart (as the unconscious out of which dreams come) was awake.

The most complete treatment of dreams in the Old Testament, however, is found in the Book of Daniel, which consists largely of a series of dreams or visions. This is one of the latest books of the Old Testament, written probably in the second century B.C. Scholars theorize that the author of the book was trying to get a message across to his people, currently struggling against the detestable oppressor Antiochus Epiphanes, who was profaning the Jewish religion. Not being able to write his message directly, the author writes a book about a Jew called Daniel who had also lived under foreign oppression during the exile in Babylonia, and beneath the dreams, visions and events of Daniel's life, there is a message for the people of the author's own time. The Book divides into two halves, each with six chapters, the first part being narrative, the second a series of visions of world-wide scope. The historicity of Daniel as a person is debated by the scholars. For our purposes, however, the point is not essential, for the fact remains that the book is a clear demonstration of the regard in which dreams were held.

Daniel is an Israelite youth of great ability. Along with three friends (Shadrach, Meshach, and Abednego) he is regarded highly for his learning, skill, and wisdom. Daniel especially had "understanding in all visions and dreams." [43]

In chapter 2 there occurs the story of Nebuchadnezzar's dream, a remarkable account in its psychological acuity. The chapter begins: "In the second year of the reign of Nebuchadnezzar, Nebuchadnezzar had dreams; and his spirit was troubled, and his sleep left him." [44] Here we have the familiar picture of a man afflicted with insomnia, which is frequently the result of conflict between the conscious and unconscious. However, during his restless sleep Nebuchadnezzar is aware of dreams. He knows he had dreams and that they were disturbing and important, but he is unable to recollect what they were. The Babylonian magicians are confronted by the King with the task of helping him, but while willing to venture an interpretation of a dream, they are unable to do so unless he can tell the dream to them. The King does not accept their ignorance of his dream as an excuse, and in his anger determines to slay all the wise men of Babylon. Daniel is included in this ultimatum, but he alone believes he might solve the King's problem and accordingly secures an appointment with Nebuchadnezzar. This done, Daniel returns to his dwelling and beseeches his comrades to "seek mercy of the God of heaven concerning this mystery. . . ." [45] And accordingly, "the mystery was revealed to Daniel in a vision of the night." [46]

Armed with this message from God, Daniel confronts the King and speaks these words:

"No wise men, enchanters, magicians, or astrologers can show to the king the mystery which the king has asked, but there is a God in heaven who reveals mysteries, and he has made known to King Nebuchadnezzar what will be in the latter days. Your dream and the visions of your head as you lay in bed are these: To you, O king, as you lay in bed came thoughts of what would be hereafter, and he who reveals mysteries made known to you what is to be. But as for me, not because of any wisdom that I have more than all the living has this mystery been revealed to me, but in order that the interpretation may be made known to the king, and that you may know the thoughts of your mind." [47]

The last phrase is especially significant to us, for it is exactly what the interpretation of a dream does for us: it reveals to us the thoughts of our unconscious mind. The word "mind" can literally stand for the word "heart." It means the inmost man, the secret thoughts and deepest emotions. It is part of the naïveté of modern man that he thinks he knows his own thoughts, when nothing is farther from the truth. We harbor thoughts in the unconscious which are not known or recognized by us, but of which we can become aware through the understanding of dreams, even as Daniel says. This is strikingly in accordance with modern psychology.

Daniel then proceeds to tell the King his dream,[48] a dream in which an image appeared wrought of many magnificent metals, but which was broken by no human hand and crumbled. Daniel gives an interpretation which clearly also contains a message for the people resisting Antiochus Epiphanes.

However, later Daniel interprets another dream of Nebuchadnezzar's which is of more psychological interest. This time Nebuchadnezzar remembers the dream and tells it to Daniel.

". . . I saw, and behold, a tree in the midst of the earth; and its height was great. The tree grew and became strong, and

DREAMS AND VISIONS IN THE BIBLE

its top reached to heaven, and it was visible to the end of the whole earth. Its leaves were fair and its fruit abundant, and in it was food for all. The beasts of the field found shade under it, and the birds of the air dwelt in its branches, and all flesh was fed from it. I saw in the visions of my head as I lay in bed, and behold, a watcher and an holy one, came down from heaven. He cried aloud and said thus, 'Hew down the tree and cut off its branches, strip off its leaves and scatter its fruit; let the beasts flee from under it and the birds from its branches. But leave the stump of its roots in the earth, bound with a band of iron and bronze, amid the tender grass of the field. Let him be wet with the dew of heaven; let his lot be with the beasts in the grass of the earth; let his mind be changed from a man's, and let a beast's mind be given to him; and let seven times pass over him. The sentence is by the decree of the watchers, the decision by the word of the holy ones, to the end that the living may know that the Most High rules the kingdom of men, and gives it to whom he will, and sets over it the lowliest of men.' " [49]

Daniel sees at once the extraordinary meaning of this dream. He finds it so dreadful that Daniel "was dismayed for a moment, and his thoughts alarmed him." [50] What follows is a sound bit of dream interpretation. The dream, Daniel warns the King, says that King Nebuchadnezzar has become like the tree, great and spacious, flowing with life and beauty. But because Nebuchadnezzar has regarded himself as the author of his power, and has assumed divine prerogatives and a godlike role, the Almighty God will cut him down. The dream is an attempt to compensate for Nebuchadnezzar's *hubris*.

Because the king does not heed the warning he loses his mind. [51] We can see this from the report about the return of his sanity. "At the end of the days I, Nebuchadnezzar, lifted my eyes to heaven, and my reason returned to me, and I blessed the Most High, and praised and honored him who lives for ever and ever. . . ." [52] Notice that Nebuchadnezzar's fate could have been averted. Daniel himself says this when he urges Nebuchadnezzar to change his ways in order "that there may perhaps be a lengthening of your tranquillity." [53] Because Nebuchadnezzar's inflexible conscious point of view about himself does not change, he has to be brought down to earth by his strange psychosis. Interestingly enough, his seven years of insanity during which he lives on the ground as a beast is directly compensating to his previous years as an exalted king. When the time has elapsed, he is restored to his reason, this time no longer afflicted by his megalomania but more truly himself. The whole story is an excellent example of the compensatory nature of the unconscious relative to the ego.

Think what a grand thing it would be if Daniel and Joseph, the interpreters of dreams, were today in the pulpits of Christendom! How alive our churches would be to the needs of the soul and the continuing revelation from God!

After all that we have heard we will not be too surprised to discover that the central experience of many Biblical figures was a dream or vision. The story of Gideon centers around a dream. In the Book of Judges, Gideon is instructed by God to go against the camp of the Midianites, and there he would be reassured by what he heard. Gideon, as he arrives there, overhears a man telling his comrade a dream:

> " 'Behold, I dreamed a dream; and lo, a cake of barley bread tumbled into the camp of Midian, and came to the tent, and struck it so that it fell, and turned it upside down, so that the tent lay flat.' And his comrade answered, 'This is not other than the sword of Gideon the son of Joash, a man

of Israel; into his hand God has given Midian and all the host.' " [54]

And the story concludes: "When Gideon heard the telling of the dream and its interpretation, he worshiped; and he returned to the camp of Israel, and said, 'Arise, for the Lord has given the host of Midian into your hand.' " [55] So began Gideon's mighty deeds, with a dream.

Most of us remember that Solomon was considered the wisest of men, but many of us have forgotten that this gift of wisdom came to Solomon through a dream. In recognition of Solomon's devotion, the Lord appeared to Solomon in a dream by night and said, "Ask what I shall give you." [56] In the account which follows Solomon asks for understanding, and God promises him the gift of a wise and discerning mind. The story concludes, "And Solomon awoke, and behold, it was a dream." [57] There is some question about how wise Solomon really was as an historical person, but it is clear how significant a dream was to the ancient author.

Turning to the New Testament, we find that at least two of the greatest religious experiences related there were visions. First there is the experience of the Transfiguration, which is concluded in Matthew's Gospel with the words spoken by our Lord: "Tell no one the vision, until the Son of man is raised from the dead." [58] Second, there is the experience of St. Paul on the road to Damascus. This was clearly of a subjective visionary nature, for only St. Paul saw it (though one source says others heard the voice). Further, in Acts,[59] Paul before Agrippa describes his vital experience as a vision. And if we only knew more of the life and personality of Pontius Pilate's wife we might find a dream at the turning point of her life too. For we remember her warning to her husband: "Have nothing to do with that righteous man, for I have suffered much over him today in a dream." [60]

Let us stop here for a moment and summarize what we have found in the Bible about dreams. We have noted some seventy passages referring to dreams and visions. On the basis of this abundant material we must conclude the following.

1. Dreams and visions were regarded in both Old and New Testaments as revelations from God. Those skilled in their interpretation, such as Daniel or Joseph, were revered; those who understood the revelations God had given them, e.g., Abraham or Solomon, became great and wise; those who were overcome by their inner experience, such as St. Paul or Ezekiel, became great missionaries and prophets.

2. Viewed from this perspective the entire Bible is the story of God's breakthrough into man's conscious mind via the unconscious.

And finally two other conclusions can be drawn which have not yet been deliberately stated:

3. that many other religious experiences, e.g., Jacob's wrestling with the adversary, or Moses' encounter with the burning bush, were of a visionary kind.

4. that the early Church regarded dreams the same way as the Bible: as revelations from God.

The men of the Bible did not first sit down to intellectualize about God. God broke through into them with a personal experience. He "convinced" them, as he did St. Paul, to use the word which literally in the Latin derivation means "to overcome." Only after their experience did the men of the Bible sit down and think about God, to give structure to and expand the meaning of their experience. First the great dreams were revelations from God. Only later were there priests and a Church to give form to the experience and to build it into ritual and dogma.

But today many of us have decided we do not want to "contaminate" our contemplation of the divine by allowing anything as nebulous and unsettling as the unconscious to intrude. We have decided that a man may find God through rational thinking, or a "group experience," or education, or formal worship, everywhere except in his own soul, which is in fact the fountainhead of religious experience. The result is that we Christians are afraid today of that very soul from which our heritage springs; we want creeds, not religious experiences, and dogma, not inspiration. Above all, we refuse to accept the nonrational unconscious, because it threatens the tyranny of rationality which has gripped us today.

We think of all sorts of excuses, of course: dealing with the unconcious, we say, is only for the mentally ill; dreams are only for the psychiatrist; revelation stopped with the New Testament, so why endanger our dogma with further revelations through dreams? In this, we differ greatly from the early Church Fathers, most of whom also declared the dream to be the Voice of God and the spiritual world. But our objections are rationalizations. The truth is, as the Epistle to the Hebrews says, "It is a fearful thing to fall into the hands of the living God." [61] We much prefer the security of our rationality to the awesome experience of dealing with a living voice.

We could of course dispense with our dreams if we wanted to, were it not for two difficulties. We could say that this belief in dreams which we see in the Bible, and in the early Church Fathers, is outmoded, a superstition, forgivable to men of ancient days but not for us enlightened

[*117*]

Christians, just as we no longer have to accept Adam and Eve as literally the first man and the first woman. Or, granting the validity of the dreams of the Bible, we could state that this was well and good but only for those times. There are only two difficulties in the way. First is the pressing need which we have today. For all of our highly sophisticated consciousness, the mind of man is sick. We need a healing, a meaning, a balance and a revelation for our minds which our rational consciousness cannot provide us. Our very urgent inner need demands that we turn again to God for revelation, if only to reveal to us as individuals what He has already revealed in the Bible, in order that we might understand it.

And secondly, we Christians discover that this neglected part of our religious life has been recognized as valuable by others in this world. Just because the churches have decided to pay no attention to their unconscious does not mean that God will stop trying to speak to men. So it is that scientific psychology and medicine, in search of a way to help men find healing and wholeness, have discovered what the Bible knew all along but Christians had forgotten: that dreams and their interpretation can heal the sick soul. Carl Jung, more perceptive and receptive than his contemporaries, has discovered that the dreams of men today are not only dreams about himself, but also about God, that in fact, at the basis of our dreams there is a religious process.

Are we not like the little boy who is afraid in his room at night and calls his mother? His mother reassures him not to be afraid, since God is there in the room with him. As the mother returns downstairs, she hears the boy say anxiously: "All right, God, it's okay for you to be here; just don't move or I'll be scared to death!" We also reassure ourselves that everything must be all right, for God is here with us,

[*118*]

and we graciously give our consent to His presence. But we add secretly: "Just don't come to us in anything as personal as a dream or an experience which really involves our personality or we will be frightened to death!"

The presence of God is a disturbing presence, especially when His voice is as close to us as our nightly dreams. We cannot deny the closeness of His presence, for we also dream dreams as did the men of the Bible. But we must look at dreams not only from the point of view of inspired intuition, as did Daniel, for instance, but also from the objective viewpoint of modern science. To this we turn in the next chapter.

VII

The Nature and Structure of Dreams

One of the most interesting experiments with sleep was recently conducted by Dr. William Dement, while he was a research fellow in psychiatry at Mount Sinai Hospital in New York City. It can now be scientifically established whether and when a man is dreaming. This can be done first because of certain movements of the eyeball under the closed eyelid, which the trained physician is able to detect, and secondly because during dreams there is a change in the brain waves of the sleeping person detectable by the electroencephalogram. With the aid of the electroencephalogram, experimenters are able to waken a person in the middle of a dream. Several experiments have revealed that all people dream on the average of about one and a half hours per eight hours of sleep, in about six or seven different dreams during the night. The person who says he does not dream simply does not remember his dreams upon awakening.

Dr. Dement went one step further, deciding to test the effect of dreams upon rest. He divided his volunteer subjects into two groups and watched during their sleep for the beginning of a dream. The persons in one group he allowed to finish dreaming, then he awakened them and let them again fall asleep. The persons of the second group he wakened immediately as a dream commenced, then he allowed them to return to sleep. In this way, both groups were awakened during the night the same approximate number of times, and at first received the same amount of total sleep, but in one group the dreams were not permitted to be completed.

Two facts emerged. First, with the second group there seemed to be a great effort on the part of the psyche to produce a dream. After the experiment had been carried on for five nights, some persons in this group tried to dream as many as thirty times during eight hours' sleep. Secondly, this group began to show on the fourth and fifth nights the same signs of mental breakdown as shown by people who have been deprived of sleep for inordinately long periods of time. Beginning with increased irritability, these people ended by having hallucinations and signs of mental breakdown. Dr. Dement concluded his talk to the American Psychiatric Association in 1960 with the following words: "We believe that if anybody were deprived of dreams long enough, it might result in some sort of catastrophic breakdown." [1] Thus one could state that Freud did not go far enough in calling dreams the guardians of sleep; Dr. Dement's data would suggest that they are "the very guardians of sanity."

Now let us turn in a systematic way to the findings of Dr. Jung, who is our psychological guide in this book. As a scientist and psychotherapist Dr. Jung observed thousands of dreams during his medical career of over half a century. While Dr. Dement devised laboratory-type experiments for his findings, Dr. Jung, being a psychotherapist interested in the healing of his patient, endeavored to deal with whatever problems his patient brought to him. His hypotheses rest consequently not upon experiments, but upon comparison of the empiric material of countless dreams and case histories, upon comparative elaborations of material found in psychoses, the life of primitive man, and other direct manifestations of man's unconscious psychic world.

All that follows is based upon the work of Dr. Jung. The presentation, however, is strictly my own. I have tried as much as possible to present his findings in a fresh and personal way. So the blame, or praise, for this rewording of Jungian ideas rests with myself. The résumé is divided into nine separate headings:

1. The Autonomy of the Dream Life
2. The Compensatory Nature of Dreams
3. The Significance of Dream Elements in General
4. The Significance of Certain Prominent Dream Figures
5. The Dream as a Cartoon or Parable
6. Nonhuman Dream Symbols, and Some Rules Guiding Dream Interpretation
7. The Transpersonal Dream Source
8. Further Description of the Collective Unconscious
9. Brief Review of the Paradoxical Nature of the Unconscious

1. The Autonomy of the Dream Life

Perhaps the first thing we notice about our dreams is their bewildering variety of images, persons, symbols and dramas. Furthermore, if as an experiment we tried to decide beforehand what we should dream we would find that our conscious will power has not the slightest effect upon the nature of our dreams. Or, should we have "decided" as an experiment that we would dream of so-and-so and so-and-so did appear in the dream, we would find that the dream had used so-and-so in a sequence or a way not previously imagined. In short, the dreams come from a source which is quite beyond our conscious control. They are "autonomous," which means that they obey their own laws. As Dr. Jung once put it: many people know that they have complexes; but few recognize the fact that the complexes *have them.*[2]

This autonomy of the unconscious psychic realm gives us a general explanation of much mental disorder. We can say in a general way that symptoms and neuroses are the result of too great a divergence between the conscious and unconscious points of view. This discrepancy leads to inner warfare, which results in a variety of symptoms the most characteristic of which is anxiety. In order to gain a better image of the range and power of the soul, let me recall the picture of an iceberg. Consciousness would correspond to the tenth of the iceberg above water, the personal unconscious to the nine tenths below the water surface, and the ocean itself to the unknown extent of the collective psyche. Clearly such a giant is not going to submit to our puny suggestions! Yet we can also speak of the two as equal partners, in the sense that each requires the other if the total psyche is to operate, for certain essential psychic functions are performed only by the ego.

To understand dreams we must approach every dream with the question, "Why did this particular dream come?" Only if we respect the autonomous powers which are expressed in the dream may we avoid the tragic fate of Nebuchadnezzar.

2. The Compensatory Nature of Dreams

A dream might compensate our conscious point of view by bringing up information we had overlooked, by hinting at unexpected solutions to problems, by showing a situation

[*123*]

in a new light, or by showing the dreamer an unrecognized aspect of himself. So in his dream a meek-minded man might see himself in a dream as Napoleon, the self-styled society woman might dream of a prostitute, and a dedicated clergyman might strangle a parishioner. In each case, through the dream an overlooked side of the dreamer's personality and situation is shown, but this side is no more the dreamer's "true" self than the everyday person whom he actually believes himself to be. The meek man is not Napoleon, the society woman is not a prostitute, and the clergyman is not a murderer. The truth lies somewhere in between.

Examples of compensatory dreams are so frequent and so rich I cannot refrain from including some more. The following short case comes from my pastoral ministry. One of the most frequent problems the pastor encounters is the person who takes his or her problem so seriously that he feels overwhelmed by his inability to work out a solution. As a matter of fact it is not easy to keep from being overwhelmed by a sense of defeat and pessimism when we look deeply into ourselves and see the enormous imperfection we all have. Pessimism is frequently a sign of our tendency to try to solve everything on a conscious level, and of our reluctance to rely upon God and the unconscious powers. Where such a conscious pessimism occurs an unconscious attitude will usually tend to compensate this one-sidedness, and such compensatory dreams are often extremely helpful in relieving the depression.

The following example came from a woman of ability and insight who had succumbed to such a pessimism regarding herself and her problems. In the midst of this pessimism she dreamt that she and her husband were removing the back from a sofa in order to carry it into a certain room in their house. When I quizzed her about this sofa I learned that she had recently purchased it secondhand, but in excellent condition, intending it for this particular room. However, she discovered that it was too large to fit through the door! For several days she and her husband had the sofa in the outer room, because not only could they not get it into its proper place but neither could they return it, for it was secondhand. I suggested on the basis of this dream that she return home and see if the back of the sofa could be detached. She did so and found to her surprise that a few simple bolts held the back in place and that once these were removed the sofa could easily be taken through the door and then reassembled!

This is a very practical dream. It is a good example of how a dream may apply to both an objective and a subjective situation, that is, to the dreamer's relationship to outer and inner reality. Many dreams, including this one, have something to say to us about our adaptation to outer life. In this case, the dream solved the practical problem. But it also had an inner, subjective meaning which is the principal concern of almost all of our dreams. It was like a voice within her saying that tasks which seem impossible to our consciousness can be quite simple if we enlist the intelligence of the unconscious. This dream impressed the dreamer greatly and gave her the encouragement she needed to pursue her inner situation towards a solution.

As a last example I will choose a dream of a compensatory nature which comes from the dialogues of Plato. In the *Phaedo* the condemned Socrates is asked by his friend Cebes, on behalf of Evenus the poet, why he has suddenly indulged in poetry with only a short time left to live. The reason which Socrates gives is a dream, which he relates as follows:

Tell him, Cebes,—he replied,—what is the truth, that I
had no idea of rivalling him or his poems; to do so, as I
knew, would be no easy task. But I wanted to see whether I
could purge away a scruple which I felt about the meaning
of certain dreams. In the course of my life, I have often had
intimations in dreams "that I should compose music." The
same dream came to me sometimes in one form and sometimes in another, but always saying the same or nearly the
same words, "Cultivate and make music," said the dream.
And hitherto I had imagined that this was only intended to
exhort and encourage me in the study of philosophy, which
has been the pursuit of my life, and is the noblest and the
best of music. The dream was bidding me do what I was
already doing, in the same way that the competitor in a race
is bidden by the spectators to run when he is already running. But I was not certain of this; for the dream might have
meant music in the popular sense of the word, and being
under sentence of death, and the festival giving me a respite,
I thought that it would be safer for me to satisfy the scruple,
and, in obedience to the dreams, to compose a few verses
before I departed.[3]

It is consistent with the greatness of Socrates that he
should recognize such a recurring dream as significant, and
—with only a short time to live—that he should do his
utmost to fulfill the dream's message. Nevertheless we can
guess that he has misinterpreted its meaning. We may reasonably assume that Plato's Socrates was a man of great
intellect, whose thinking function, or intellectual abilities,
had been developed to their maximum. We know that such
a person often suffers from an underdevelopment of his
feelings. That something of this sort had happened with
Socrates is substantiated by what we know of his relationship with his family, which was at the best not close. When
the dream says, "Socrates, play music," it tries to compen-

sate for his one-sided intellectual development by urging him to cultivate his irrational feeling qualities.

3. The Significance of Dream Figures in General.

In order to comprehend the meaning of our various dream figures we must realize that our dreams are almost invariably a reproduction of our own inner situation. Dreams are primarily about the personality of the dreamer himself; they are not about external matters except as they relate to that personality. Now there are exceptions,[4] but they are rare, and we can say as a general rule that every dream is about the dreamer, his own problems, and his own relationship to himself and his world.

If, for example, we should dream of the end of the world, it would be madness to assume that this must be a vision of the imminent end to the actual, physical world. It is our inner world that is meant by the dream, and the dream concerns a momentous change which is taking place in us. Or if Uncle Joe should die in our dream, let us not rush and inform him of his coming catastrophe. For the dream is not about Uncle Joe but about ourselves, and the death will not be his but the death of something within us which he represents.

Our hypothesis of an unconscious psychic realm asserts that much of our psychic life goes on without our awareness. The dream provides a means for us to glimpse into this unconscious life of the psyche by presenting a picture of the inner situation. Looking at a dream is like looking out of the window of a bathysphere at the wonders that exist under the sea. During sleep our consciousness is in a bathysphere immersed in the oceanic depths of the unconscious. What we see here is reality *within ourselves*.

Let us now consider our dream as a dramatic production.

The scene is laid in a certain place, the curtain goes up, and actors and actresses become animated. Even though upon awakening everything that happens might appear senseless, now it all seems reasonable enough. One of the first questions we will want to ask is, "What do these actors and actresses want? Who are they and what do they signify?" The number of them seems to be bewildering and their identification often difficult, since we meet among them many strangers as well as people known to us from our conscious life.

But fortunately there is a meaning to the multiplicity of these "dramatis personae" of our nightly drama, for they represent aspects or tendencies of the dreamer himself. We can say as a general rule that the people who appear in our dreams represent aspects or fragments of our own personality, and the reason that so many people appear in a course of dreams is to be found in the complexity of human nature. We are not the simple, uncomplicated people we would like to suppose. Each one of us contains the capacity or potential for every emotion or tendency found in the human race. We are saints and sinners, prophets and criminals, feminine and masculine all rolled into one.

Jung's theory of the complexes explains why in dreams autonomous parts of our personality appear as separate figures. During our development some of these are made conscious, and some remain unconscious. These unconscious personality components do not cease to exist, but lead a life of their own in the background of the psyche, from where they exert pronounced effects upon our conscious life.

Suppose we would have refused to recognize hate in ourselves. Our hateful side would not cease to exist. For nothing of the psyche can ever be eliminated. All continues to live in our unconscious. Then we might dream of an unknown dark and vicious man (if we are men) or woman (if we are women), some person known to us who is outspoken in his hostile feelings. Such a figure represents our own hostile side, which lives a life of its own, and "asks" through the dream for recognition by our conscious personality. Because of their autonomy and the complexity of emotion surrounding them Jung calls such representations "Autonomous Complexes."

A complex often reveals itself in strange ways. I recall the good Christian woman who was telling me of a quarrel with her neighbor, (whom she "loved with Christian love" of course) and she said to me: "I spoke venomently to her" (intending to say "vehemently"). She herself remained unaware of the slip which she had made and I did not try to enlighten her, but it was evident that her own unconscious venomous side had intruded momentarily into her speech. Someone "other" than her ego had spoken through her.

Now such an idea sounds a bit frightening, and in fact it is an alarming thought. For these autonomous complexes can become dangerous fellows if matters get out of hand and we have not given them any recognition. They can be responsible for split personality, flashes of anger, moodiness, momentary amnesia, embarrassing slips of the tongue, errors, accident proneness, and so forth. The psyche is a bundle of such complexes. So it is entirely natural for us to share our psychic home with these bedfellows who appear in our dreams. Fortunately we can establish harmony with them if we make the necessary effort.

4. The Significance of Certain Prominent Dream Figures

In spite of the great variety of dream figures, there are certain typical ones among them which occur with unusual frequency. Through this, and through their decisive influence upon the happenings of the dreams, we know that these typical figures must be particularly important to our psychology. Such figures Dr. Jung has called "archetypes." One may explain them as follows: because we are human we have certain basic personality components, common to all men. An archetype represents such a basic part of human nature. If, for instance, we were going to produce an old-time Western drama it would be necessary to have certain persons in our story, such as a hero, a heroine, and a villain. We might or might not include other persons as well, but these three are essential. Similarly, if we are to have a human being we must have certain important components to his total character—otherwise he would not be human: he might be a devil, or an angel, or a fairy or goblin, but he would not be human. The archetypal figures can be thought of as the "basic cast of characters" making up the personality of every human being. There are many such archetypal figures, but I will only mention a few of the most important ones.

The first of these archetypal dream figures I will describe is the "shadow" or "alter ego," whom we have already met in Chapter I. If a man stands facing the light, he will cast a shadow. But unless he turns and looks on the floor behind him he will not be aware of the dark shadow following him. The shadow is the dark part of our personality, which is in our background, of which we are usually unaware. He is that part of us which our conscious mind can only accept with difficulty. So he is our angry side, our weakness, our sickness, our primitiveness, our sensuality, our rebelliousness or inferiority, whatever it may be about ourselves of which we are most afraid and would rather not face.

Where do we see the shadow? He appears in our dreams

as a sinister or inferior figure of our own sex. We may also find him standing between our intentions and our achievement, in the projections we make upon people of our own sex, at the root of much racial prejudice, at the bottom of many of our broken human relationships. The more we try to remain unaware of him, the more he manifests himself to us in these ways.

We can understand him in contrast to the "persona." The persona is the mask which we wear before the world; it is the front we put on. Partly the persona is a matter of social necessity, a form of adaption to the society in which we live. But too often we come to identify ourselves with our persona. We think we are the person whom we would like to appear to be. The shadow stands in direct contrast to this persona. The more we try to appear all goodness and kindness, the more brutal our shadow appears in contrast; the more we try to be all strength and courage, the more we are followed by a shadow of weakness.

Partly the qualities of the shadow are individually colored depending on the nature of our consciousness, on that which is repressed into the personal unconscious, and on the particular kind of persona we have adopted. But partly the shadow is also a cultural phenomenon, and shows what is neglected or repressed in the entire culture in which we live as well as in our individual life. In an era like ours, for instance, which emphasizes the intellect, education, sophistication of manners and morals, the collective shadow is the neglected primitive man in us.

There is no human being without a shadow, since the ego in its adjustment to life necessarily identifies with certain components of the personality at the expense of others which are left in an unconscious condition.

All of this makes the shadow seem a sinister figure. Of

[*131*]

course the more unconscious we are of our shadow the more autonomous and undifferentiated is his behavior within us. Then he is likely to erupt with violently disturbing manifestations, or he can place himself—an unseen entity—between our intentions and our achievements. But when the shadow is given conscious recognition we will find that he has much of positive value to add to our personality, often giving us that earthiness, or instinctuality, or zest for living, or humility, which is exactly what we need to complement our personality and become a complete human being. It is a strange thing about the shadow: for all of his darkness, he seems close to God. So it is that when we begin to wrestle with our shadow, we find ourselves—like Jacob—somehow also wrestling with God. Seeing our shadow, the "beam that is in our own eye," is essential to religious experience, the beginning of a confrontation with ourselves and with God.

A second recurring dream figure is peculiar to masculine psychology. Just as a man will notice an inferior masculine figure reappearing in his dreams, so he will notice the recurrence of one or a variety, of feminine figures who seem in the dream to exert a curiously compelling influence. To understand this woman in our dreams, we must revert to our thesis that a human being is a full measure of all human possibilities. So a man has feminine components as well as masculine components to his personality. Now most men, because of the influence of their physiology, the pressure of society, and the need to establish a masculine ego position, identify with their masculine component. As a result the masculine personality traits are more or less well developed, and the ego thinks of itself as masculine. What happens to the neglected feminine components? They constellate themselves as an "inner woman," they become a woman within the man, and appear in dreams in the shape of female figures.

This "inner woman" Jung has termed the "anima." In the psychology of the man she is an important part of his soul, his lost other half, an inner being who animates him and fills him with life. Like any woman, she personifies eros and emotionality. She is also an intermediary for him with the outside world of relationships on the one hand, and the world of the unconscious on the other hand. She fills the man with sexual feelings and tensions, with lust and desire for the material world. But she also has an important religious function, connecting the man's understanding with that which is real and divine. Jung has gone so far as to say that the anima is to God as the eye is to the sun. What Tertullian writes of the soul applies equally to the anima: "Though under the oppressive bondage of the body, though led astray by depraving customs, though enervated by lusts and passions, though in slavery to false gods; yet, whenever the soul comes to itself, as out of a surfeit, or a sleep, or a sickness, and attains something of its natural soundness, it speaks of God." [5]

Whether she is helpful or destructive in the man's life will depend upon the relationship which exists between the masculine ego and the erotic, tender, emotional, feminine side of himself which the anima personifies. When a man is in good relationship with her, she fills him with positive attributes of loyalty, love, and relatedness to people and to the unconscious, and actually increases his masculine strength by giving him emotional support. When he is not related to her, she will tend to "possess" him, filling him with irrational moods, causing him to sulk, become embittered or pessimistic. In extreme cases the ego may identify with her, and sexual aberrations are a consequence.

[*133*]

The anima is not just an idea. She is discernible in dreams, in masculine behavior, and in literature. We will see her in our dreams now as mother, then as sweetheart, as the image of the soul, as seductress, as witch, as spiritual guide, as a little child, as a divine woman. In our life she is our inspiration, our dark mood, our tenderness, our relatedness to people, that which we project onto actual women and love in them, someone who embroils us in womanish irrationality, someone who lifts us to God. She is partly the net result of our contacts with women in our life, especially childhood contacts with the mother; but she is also like all the other women who have ever lived. She may bear the marks of our personal life but she is also just "Woman."

In literature she is Dante's Beatrice, Homer's Helen of Troy, Goethe's Gretchen. In short, she is to be found wherever men are led and guided by the feminine spirit. Through her, men can know and understand what a woman is like. The anima is an enormously important aspect of masculine psychology. The discovery of this woman in a man is a unique and important contribution of Jung to our understanding of ourselves.

The astute woman reader may now guess for herself the third recurring archetypal figure: it is the man in her dreams, a peculiarity of the psychology of women, whom Jung has called the "animus." His existence can be explained in a similar way as the existence of the anima in the man. He represents the woman's own neglected masculine qualities, forms a separate personality within her, and exerts a great influence upon the woman's consciousness. He acts as spokesman for some of her unconscious attitudes and is the woman's lost spirit. He holds the key to the woman's development as a person in her own right. The more she wishes to become an individual, and not just Eve, the mother of the race, the more must she recognize and develop the animus.

Like the anima, the animus is seen in dreams, in the behavior of women, and in literature. In her dreams he is father, husband, lover, spiritual guide, healer, sorcerer, demon, any one of scores of kinds of men. In her behavior he is just as variable. He may help her to constructive thinking, individual development, creative ideas, or fill her with inflexible opinions, sever her relationships to people, give her a biting tongue, or become a tormenting voice which tells her what she must be thinking and doing. Just as the man will see his anima reflected in a woman and will come to understand women through the anima, so a woman will see her animus reflected in a man and through him she can understand what a man is like. Whether he is devil or spiritual guide, irrational opinion or inner lover, will depend upon the woman's relationship to him.

In literature the animus is not so prevalent as the anima for the simple reason that most literature is written by men. But an excellent example of the animus is Heathcliff in Emilie Bronte's *Wuthering Heights*. From the Apocrypha, Asmodeus, the demon in the Book of Tobit, is a striking example.

I will comment upon only one more recurring dream figure: the dreamer himself. It is interesting that almost invariably the dreamer himself appears in the dream, if not in the action then at least as a spectator. This, if nothing else, should convince us of the intensely personal nature of the dream. I can recall the first dream my daughter reported at the age of four. She rushed into the breakfast room one morning, eyes wide with excitement, and announced: "Mother, I had a story last night; it was a bear story—and I was in it too!" What does it mean that we ourselves should appear in our dreams? It means exactly what it says: that consciousness is involved in what is going on, for we stand in the dream for the ego. This poses the question of the relation between the ego and the unconscious.

At birth the entire psyche, that is, the total psychic organism of personality, is unconscious. There is psychic life in the infant, but there is no sense of identity, nothing but instinctive response. Very soon, however, parents begin to recognize a glimmering of awareness: the infant "recognizes" mother, when she comes into the room, he smiles. Before too long the signs are unmistakable: an ego has emerged out of the unconsciousness. Now the child recognizes the parents and the environment; memory has awakened. Soon the child will become aware of his own identity and the continuity of his experience. This is one reason why small children are so jealous of their name. "My name is not Joannie, it's Sally," the little girl is likely to say adamantly should we mistake her identity. The child tries to defend zealously its young and precious consciousness of identity. Unfortunately for mother and father, the ego at this point is weak. For this reason the small child is subject to irrational moods and whims, to which it holds with astonishing stubbornness. We are apt to mistake this stubbornness for willfulness; it is, however, simply a sign of the weakness of the ego in the face of the unconscious. In fact, parents will find during this period that they themselves act as the ego of the child: "Don't cross the street; look out for cars; remember, dear, fire hurts; if you pull the kitty's tail he will scratch you." In countless scores of ways the parents supply the protective and supporting functions of the ego for the child.

Nevertheless, the ego has been born, and out of unconsciousness the tiny seed of consciousness continues to sprout. Just as a flower emerges from the ground first as a tender bud, then only gradually grows to full strength, so the human ego emerges first weak and susceptible to all manner of psychic influences before it slowly grows to the full strength and scope of maturity. This emergence of the ego, with its self-awareness and eventually its "knowledge of good and evil," looks like an emergence from the paradise of nature. Adam and Eve upon eating the fruit "know" for the first time and this knowledge brings about their banishment from paradise.

It is this conscious ego-part of ourselves which we usually think of as "I." While there are aspects of the ego unknown to the ego itself, yet roughly we may say that our ego is more or less identical with our consciousness. Thus when we see ourselves portrayed in the dream we are looking at the portrayal of our consciousness or ego.[6] And by observing what happens to us in our dreams we can learn a great deal about the essential matter of the relationship between the ego and the unconscious psyche.

This brief resume is only an introduction to vast areas of the psyche. But perhaps we have been given enough information to at least identify the principal characters of our dreams. We are now in a position to gain further insights into the nature of the dream by comparing it to things familiar to us all: the cartoon and the parable.

5. The Dream as a Cartoon or Parable

In a cartoon a truth is expressed from the point of view of the cartoonist. The cartoonist employs symbolic language, both in words and images. When the reader gets the point of the cartoon he finds that it contains in a nutshell the very essence of a situation.

Suppose, for instance, we saw a picture of a round, globelike little man with a worried expression on his face, looking apprehensively at two figures, one with a hammer and sickle on his shirt, the other an Uncle Sam, each of them saying, "Let us have peace" but each of them holding a rocket behind his back. The cartoon-picture would immediately be clear to the modern reader as a picture of world anxiety over the two giants, the Soviet Union and the United States, who talk peace but arm for war. If, however, a man from Mars were to look at the cartoon he could not understand it until he learned about the planet earth. In the world of dreams we are much like the man from Mars, for the unconscious presents symbolic pictures to us in dreams in a way much like the cartoon. When we understand the language employed, it is a marvel of clarity and brevity; when we do not, it is obscure. So our task is not to accuse the unconscious of malicious intent to deceive, but to ask ourselves how we may come to understand the language of the Soul.

In a similar way the dream is like a parable, the way of teaching which our Lord Himself used when he wanted to teach some especially important spiritual truth. For instance, when He spoke about the Kingdom of God, which evidently is a reality, but apprehensible only by the spiritual understanding, He said: "[It] is like a merchant in search of fine pearls, who, on finding one pearl of great value, went and sold all that he had and bought it." [7] By using a parable He was not trying to be evasive, to the contrary, He was trying to be as clear as possible. But the subject was of such a nature that it could not be communicated directly, but only in symbolic or metaphoric form. The understanding of the parable was open to all those with spiritual understanding, but not to the literally minded. So our Lord frequently says, "He who has ears to hear, let him hear."

6. Nonhuman Dream Symbols, and Some Rules Guiding Dream Interpretation

Dreams contain not only human figures, but also all manner of animal figures, inanimate objects, and natural occurrences. In dreams we might encounter snakes, birds, horses, bulls, spiders, beetles, lions, tigers, dinosaurs, cats, dogs, or mice, just to mention some of the most common animal forms. Likewise we may dream of a body of water, ice, snow, a house, road, woods, swamps, sun, moon, stars, a car, a ball—the list could be expanded almost endlessly. Or again, we may find ourselves involved in some natural occurrence, such as an earthquake, a fire, a wind, or some similar disturbance. And here is the point which should be stressed: it is impossible to catalogue these varying symbols under stereotyped meanings. We cannot say: water means always this, and lion can only stand for that. Even if the most complete "dictionary" of dream symbols were drawn up enabling us to look up any particular symbol in order to get its meaning, the attempt would not only be futile but utterly misleading. For every dream is a unique and spontaneous creation of the psyche, and the psyche is capable of using anything to mean anything. The only exceptions to this rule are certain symbols of the collective unconscious, which tend to reappear with the same general significance. But even here we must be careful, for the psyche is not bound by any rules, and even the archetypal dream symbol's meaning may vary considerably, according to the personality of the dreamer and his unique circumstances.

Then how can we ever establish the meaning of a dream?

Many things are necessary for the understanding of dreams. It is reassuring to remember that the dream, in its own way, is saying exactly what it means; it is not trying to veil or conceal anything from consciousness, quite to the contrary, it may be "hoping" for the understanding of consciousness. And while there are no stereotyped meanings to dreams, there are some guidelines we can follow.

First, we must acquaint ourselves with the dreamer's conscious situation. Such questions as, What kind of person is dreaming this dream? What is his age and circumstance in life? What are the immediate life problems with which he is dealing? What is his profession? What was he doing or what happened to him the day or days immediately preceding? The answer to any or all of these questions might be essential to understanding the dream, for a dream makes sense only in the context of a person's life.

Secondly, the understanding may require a study of not only one dream, but of several dreams. Often we are able to see what a particular dream is getting at only when we have seen a whole series of dreams. In fact, it is not an uncommon experience to study a dream, arrive only at very inconclusive interpretations, merely to discover the full meaning maybe months later in the light of some new insights about oneself.

Our unconscious life is like a continuous movie of which each dream is only an isolated scene. Therefore to break in suddenly into the inner drama by being presented with just one dream is like getting into the middle of a movie. Now in some movies we might be able to see immediately what is happening, but other movies might baffle us, so that we would say, "Let's wait and see what happens next."

Thirdly, we should have associations about the dream material from the dreamer himself. If the dreamer dreams of Mr. Jones we will certainly want to know what the dreamer feels about Mr. Jones. If he dreams of a house where he once lived, we will need to know the circumstances of his life in this previous abode.

Fourthly, the art of dream interpretation can only be cultivated through extensive personal experience with one's own dreams. Only firsthand knowledge of ourselves and our dream life, with the help of a trained expert in the field, can give us the insight which is required in order to follow their bewildering complexity.

Finally, we will need as much erudition as possible to understand those dreams which come from the transpersonal source of the collective unconscious. The symbols used in such a dream will not be available to us through the personal associations of the dreamer because they do not come from the personal layer of the psyche. To understand the symbols of a dream from the transpersonal psyche we must find their parallels in religions and mythologies.

Why should a myth be helpful to us in understanding a dream? Because a myth is a collective dream. A myth portrays a stage of psychological development universal to all men; it is a landmark in human development. So it is the "dream" of a whole people. Today each individual psyche goes through the stages of psychic transformation which men have experienced throughout their history. Like Perseus who slew the Gorgon, so every child must slay the deadly dragon of the unconscious all over again and free his ego from the coils of the unconscious. In the case of a fundamental psychic crisis, when we are blocked at a vital stage of transformation in life, then the collective unconscious is likely to be constellated, producing a dream of archetypal character. In such cases a thorough understanding of man's history, myths, and religions will be of more

[*141*]

value than anything else to help us see which myth the individual is now living.

7. The Transpersonal Dream Source

Let us now contrast personal dream material with the dream of a man about fifty years of age, known to me through my parish ministry. He had never concerned himself with dreams, or with psychology; he is a matter-of-fact, down-to-earth person, with an assertive personality and a well-developed ego. The following dream made such an impression upon him that he came to see me to discuss it. I asked him to record his experience in writing.

> Three times, in related and connecting sequences, have I dreamed of the presence of a dark shadow. The first two are so vivid that even at this date, over two years later, it is—and I write with frank candor—difficult, if not impossible, for me to discount or pass them from memory as a pure figmentation of the subconscious. Some time during the night of my first encounter with the dark shadow I awakened and without knowing why or having any intelligent reason or purpose, slipped out of bed and seemingly with no physical exertion on my part hurried out of the bedroom and down the hall to my left, towards the front room. Upon entering it I quickly made a speedy and complete circle, counterclockwise, of the room, bending over and sniffing with the alacrity of an excited hound dog on a keen spoor. I am still aware of the intense intake of my nostrils as I completed the circle. I then promptly returned to the bedroom and paused at the foot of my bed. Something was wrong, I sensed it. Yet, I had detected nothing amiss; nevertheless, I was not satisfied and somewhat perplexed, cautiously returned to the hallway door. This time I halted and looked down the hall in the opposite direction to my right, where it joins with the kitchen and bathroom. And now the

muscles in my whole body snapped tight and became taut, for I saw a dark intruder. I watched every one of his movements as a wild animal watches its unsuspecting prey before it springs for the kill. He entered the bathroom, went to the toilet bowl, faced it, as if to urinate. With incredible speed I sprinted down the hall into the bathroom and with arm stretched out leaped into the air to fall upon my intended victim and bring him to the floor. At this instant I awoke.

My first reaction was total bewilderment, for I seldom ever recall a dream and if I do, it is only with a faint recollection which is usually incomplete and abruptly terminates. This dream to me, however, was quite startling and almost real. After much deliberation and being still as bewildered as when I awoke I turned over in bed, disgusted that I had wasted my time. I recall remarking to myself that if nothing else, at least, I had been a man and went after the intruder. This thinking pacified me greatly and being well pleased with myself fell sound asleep. Upon awakening the next morning the first thing that entered my consciousness was the dark intruder. He lingered in my thoughts off and on during the day and then later, as my interest dissipated, he passed from my mind into oblivion.

The second encounter was two or three nights later. In this dream I was suddenly wide awake. He stood in the bedroom doorway sharply silhouetted against the soft glow of the night light in the bathroom. His eyes were fixed directly on mine piercing the very depth of my soul. I was held spellbound as though in a trance. I could not move, could not think or cry out, my strength had perished, only my eyes were functioning, but they were solely dominated by his penetrating eyes which held me firmly, as if by hypnosis, in his resolute command. I was terrified, utterly helpless. The intruder did not move, did not speak, he stood there in the doorway with eyes burning into mine. I remained petrified in that same, frightful, rigid, deathlike condition. At last—after what even now seems of infinite duration—he vanished; the doorway was empty. At once all my faculties were restored. I had the sensation of a numb ache in my legs just above the knees. I moved them slightly, the ache slowly disappeared and I felt that vitality was returning. I rolled on my back and raised my arms. I was greatly disturbed and then, in a fit of anger at the hellish state I had been subjugated to, I said, "The beast returned to show me that he was the master and not I." To this statement, I hastily conceded without argument. Then I returned to sleep.

As best I can recount, it was well over a year before I encountered the dark shadow again. This time it was not so vivid or alive. This dream would hardly have remained in my memory, except for my previous two encounters with the dark shadow.

Early in the evening I had attended a private gathering of friends to hear a tape recording on the subject, Religious Healing. The speaker was a well-known author and lecturer, recognized as such by accredited accomplishment in that field. On my way home I did considerable thinking on some of the salient points of the lecture when the dark shadow crept into and obsessed my thoughts. Suppose I met the dark intruder again—maybe tonight! This thought gripped my attention, I most certainly had no desire to meet him again under similar circumstances like the last time. Nevertheless, I found myself looking forward to a third meeting with fortified anticipation even to the extent that I purposely faced the hallway door when I retired and stretching out quietly, I watched with stealthy, barely opened eyes. Eventually sleep overpowered me. I remember muttering to myself, "How stupid: if and when he comes it will not be at my will but his." I accepted this as sound reasoning and was soon fast asleep, I dreamed that I was in the front room struggling desperately and silently with him at the very point where I had commenced making a complete circle a year before. I had no sense of physical contact with the intruder and the engagement was brief, but while it lasted I had the feeling that slowly I was gaining the upper hand. I awoke, somewhat disappointed, but relieved, that the fight had been going in my favor, at least, according to my impression.

I thought: "It is conceivable that the dark shadow and I shall have a rendezvous again; if so, I hope on an amiable basis."

This dream invites comparison with two passages from the Bible: The first is the story of Jacob's wrestling with God's angel, or with God himself—a story mentioned before.[8]

Can we fail to notice parallels between Jacob's experience and the dream more than three thousand years later of an American Christian? In both a dark adversary appears, there is a wrestling match requiring great courage on the part of the human individual. Jacob's adversary refuses to give his name, but is identified in the Bible as God Himself. We suspect, then, that our dreamer may have encountered God in the form of "the Presence."

Now compare the dreams with this passage from Job:

> "Now a word was brought to me stealthily,
>   my ear received the whisper of it.
> Amid thoughts from visions of the night,
>   when deep sleep falls on men,
> dread came upon me, and trembling,
>   which made all my bones shake.
> A spirit glided past my face;
>   the hair of my flesh stood up.
> It stood still,
>   but I could not discern its appearance.

[145]

> A form was before my eyes;
>   there was silence, then I heard a voice:
> 'Can mortal man be righteous before God?' " [9]

The parallels are unmistakable. There is a nameless form or presence, a spirit but with the outline and voice of a man. It is the Lord Himself who speaks, and the human being is benumbed with terror at the approach of the Nameless One. In the first and third dreams of our contemporary, we have a close parallel to Jacob's experience; in the second we have a striking parallel to an ancient dream from the Book of Job!

What are we to say of such dreams? They came quite spontaneously to a conventional person, who had no knowledge of psychology. Had we asked the dreamer, "Do you know anyone of whom this figure reminds you?," he would have been at a loss to answer. It was not like anything in the dreamer's personal experience. But when we discover the resemblance between these dreams and a dream thousands of years before then we begin to wonder: has the dream emerged from a deeper unconscious level than the personal level? Are we dealing here with an oft-repeated, therefore archetypal, confrontation of man with God which transcends the human personality of the dreamer? In short, in this dream do we see a meeting between the individual, limited mind of the dreamer, and the transpersonal mind of God? And is this the reason why such a dream always brings with it a numinous feeling, i.e., a feeling of having confronted something dreadfully, wonderfully holy or awesome?

In order to answer just such questions, Carl Jung postulated the existence of a transpersonal level of the unconscious, which he called the collective unconscious. When Freud first conceived of the unconscious it was for him the area of forgotten or repressed memories and emotions of one's own personal life. What Jung means by the unconscious realm of the psyche is best explained by his own words.

But as to whether this supra-individual psychic activity actually exists, I have so far given no proof that satisfies all the requirements. I should now like to do this once more in the form of an example. The case is that of a man in his thirties, who was suffering from a paranoid form of schizophrenia. He became ill in his early twenties. He had always presented a strange mixture of intelligence, wrong-headedness, and fantastic ideas. He was an ordinary clerk, employed in a consulate. Evidently as a compensation for his very modest existence he was seized with megalomania and believed himself to be the Saviour. He suffered from frequent hallucinations and was at times very much disturbed. In his quiet periods he was allowed to go unattended in the corridor. One day I came across him there, blinking through the window up at the sun, and moving his head from side to side in a curious manner. He took me by the arm and said he wanted to show me something. He said I must look at the sun with eyes half shut, and then I could see the sun's phallus. If I moved my head from side to side, the sun-phallus would move too, and that was the origin of the wind.

I made this observation about 1906. In the course of the year 1910 when I was engrossed in mythological studies, a book of Dieterich's came into my hands. It was part of the so-called Paris magic papyrus and was thought by Dieterich to be a liturgy of the Mithraic cult. It consisted of a series of instructions, invocations, and visions. One of these visions is described in the following words: "And likewise the so-called tube, the origin of the ministering wind. For you will see hanging down from the discus of the sun, something that looks like a tube. And towards the regions westward it is as though there were an infinite east wind. But if the other

[*147*]

wind should prevail towards the regions of the east, you will in like manner see the vision veering in that direction." The Greek word for "tube" (aulos) means a wind instrument, and the combination "aulos-paxus" in Homer means a "thick jet of blood." So evidently a stream of wind is blowing through the tube out of the sun.

The vision of my patient in 1906, and the Greek text first edited in 1910, should be sufficiently far apart to rule out the possibility of cryptomnesia on his side and of thought transference on mine. The obvious parallelism of the two visions cannot be disputed, though one might object that the similarity is purely fortuitous. In that case we should expect the vision to have no connections with analogous ideas, nor any inner meaning. But this expectation is not fulfilled, for in certain medieval paintings this tube is actually depicted as a sort of hose-pipe reaching down from heaven under the robe of Mary. In it the Holy Ghost flies down in the form of a dove to impregnate the Virgin. As we know from the miracle of Pentecost, the Holy Ghost was originally conceived as a mighty, rushing wind, the pneuma, "the wind that bloweth where it listeth" (see John 3). In a Latin text we read: "Animo descensus per orbem solis tributuir" (they say that the spirit descends through the disc of the sun). This conception is common to the whole of late classical and medieval philosophy.

I cannot, therefore, discover anything fortuitous in these visions, but simply the revival of possibilities of ideas that have always existed, that can be found again in the most diverse minds and in all epochs, and are therefore not to be mistaken for inherited ideas.

I have purposely gone into the details of this case in order to give you a concrete picture of that deeper psychic activity which I call the Collective Unconscious. Summing up, I would like to emphasize that we distinguish three psychic levels: (1) consciousness, (2) the personal unconscious, and (3) the collective unconscious.[10]

We must not suppose of course that Jung rests his whole argument for the Collective Unconscious on this single instance. This is only one of the untold numbers of dreams and visions which have brought Jung to this conclusion.[11]

8. Further Description of the Collective Unconscious

We seldom find in actual practice dreams which we can say are purely personal or purely collective. The personal unconscious can be said to consist mainly of the memories, emotions, incidents, impressions, impulses, and so forth, which one has repressed, of which one is consequently unaware, but which are peculiar to the person's individual life and experience. A forgotten or repressed incident of childhood, for instance, would belong to the sphere of the personal unconscious, or a psychologically undigested sexual episode might be an example. The collective unconscious on the other hand consists of the basic psychic impulses and potentialities of the human race.

In one way the collective unconscious must be understood in terms of the past. We have already noted at our discussion of myths that in the course of time the psyche has undergone a process of transformation.[12] In this evolution of the psyche the originally limited ego of primitive man, with its twilight consciousness, and constant proximity to a devouring unconscious matrix, has become the highly differentiated ego consciousness of today's western man. The forms along which this transformation took place are contained in man's myths and religions. If we wanted to travel by train from one point to another, we would need a railroad track. Similarly, psychic transformation needs a track along which psychic energy can flow to achieve a new goal. These "forms" or "tracks" continue to live on in us in the collective unconscious, and should our inner development become blocked, or should we confront a particularly significant human situation such as death, it may constellate a dream with mythological characteristics. Because these dreams are typical of the human situation we call them archetypal.

But it would be a mistake to understand the collective unconscious only in terms of the past, for it may also have a striving toward future goals and developments not yet realized. As we study a series of dreams we find ourselves asking: "What is the unconscious driving at?" The way in which our dreams show the problems confronting the personality, by bringing up unconscious material and consistently compensating the conscious viewpoint, enables us to work toward the wholeness of our personality, and this in turn makes us feel as if our dreams had a sense of purpose. Do we see in the psyche a mere "history" of the race and the individual, or also a pattern for the future of the individual, a pattern unknown to consciousness but known to the deeper stratas of the unconscious? At this point in our knowledge it is hard to state definitely to what extent we are justified in calling the unconscious psyche "purposive." But it is clear that something unconsciously guides us into our future development, and that a human being is affected from within not only by something "pushing from behind," but also by something trying to lead into the future.

Let me use two illustrations. Those readers who know Plato will remember his thoughts of a world of "ideas" or "forms" and his thesis that the actual, created world took its existence from these forms or ideas. So there was the Form or Idea of the Tree, and individual trees took their essence from this archetypal Tree. In some such manner it can be said we unconsciously contain an image of what we should become, and the psyche tries to lead each individual human being to fulfill this destiny. Or, to put it another way, it is as though there lived in us the one whom God has in mind. Imagine the Creator having an image of us in His mind when we are created: we have not yet grown into that image. But our unconscious seems to contain the knowledge of this "divine man," as well as the capacity to realize him in us.

Perhaps we can see now that the unconscious world in us is both "below" and "above." The unconscious does contain material which could be described as "lower." This is in the basement of the mind, where lower and inferior contents of the personality are discarded. But it also contains "heaven," including the "higher personality" which strives to be realized. So our dreams abound with the images of God as Creator, with the impact of God as Redeemer, and with the influences of what must be called the Holy Spirit. They also abound with a host of other religious influences from lesser-known religions, and an abundance of ideas and images from the great myths of mankind.

In spite of the higher and lower psychic realms within us, we must not rashly try to make a separation into two compartments. The psyche is a whole, a unity, containing many varieties. In a dream we might find the most gross personal contents mingled with images of God. The man who hopes to deal with the things of God without dealing with his own dirty laundry is doomed to failure.

Our exploration of the collective unconscious is just beginning, and in this inner world of man we stand at a virgin frontier.

9. Summary of the Paradoxical Nature of the Unconscious

The dream is a spontaneous product of the unconscious psyche. It has the function of maintaining the psychic balance and of furthering the growth of the individual. The language of the dream seems obscure to us because it is not the language of the conscious mind. The dream does not speak in scientific, rational terms, but uses the language of symbol, of myth, and of parable, and expresses itself through something that resembles an inner drama, a sketch, or a cartoon. It shows a view of the inner dreamer's situation; it emphasizes certain aspects, with the apparent intention of compensating a deficiency in the conscious viewpoint.

The study of the dream shows us that man is composed of both a conscious and unconscious mental component, each with its function and point of view, and that—in spite of its seemingly chaotic nature—the unconscious realm contains within itself a certain intelligence of its own. We can describe this relationship between the conscious and unconscious parts of the psyche as a dialogue, or discussion, *auseinandersetzung* in German, a word that implies "taking apart," "clarifying" as well as "confrontation." Two psychic principles are having a running conversation, and the result is a dialectical process in which they influence each other.

So the psyche can best be described in paradoxes. The unconscious realm which contains the refuse of our lives also contains the image of heavenly realities. Besides the effect of the past it also contains the image of the future. In spite of the chaotic multiplicity of varying tendencies, it also contains the image of wholeness and a tendency to work for the completeness of the personality. In our unconscious inner world we find higher and lower, heaven and hell, spirit and matter, combined in a paradoxical unity. Anyone who tries to reduce the psyche to rational simplic-

[*152*]

ity will miss its essence. It is as complex and paradoxical as life itself.

The dream expresses all of these varying aspects of unconscious psychic reality. It reveals through its sequence of images a kind of purposiveness at work which can only be described as religious, since it seeks to relate man to life and to his wholeness. When consciousness is at war with what is unconscious, when there is conflict because these two points of view have separated too far, then there is discord in the personality. But when the conscious and unconscious points of view are brought closer together, and a relationship or harmony is established, then there emerges a possibility for the wholeness which God has destined for each man.

Our remaining two chapters will be concerned with this wholeness, the problems we confront in trying to achieve it, and how our dreams must be regarded as the Voice of our Creator.

VIII

The Christian Problem

1

We will now turn to a problem which plays a major part in our dreams. Because it is so typical in our Western Christian culture, I have called it "the Christian problem." We will begin with a concrete example of how this problem can affect our lives. Then we shall study it in the Bible and in early Christian history, and finally we shall observe how modern dreams are working on a solution of this problem.

Doris, as we shall call her, about fifty years of age, unmarried, poorly paid employee of a technical enterprise, came to see me. She explained that she had come because of her depression and her unhappy history; she hoped I could show her where to find God. She told me how she awoke in the morning with no energy, forced herself to go to work, returned home with no desire to see anyone, and occasionally succumbed to fear that a previous illness would return. This previous illness had occurred a year or so ago and resulted in her being sent to a state hospital; her depression had given way to its opposite, and during a sudden eruption of energy she had made extravagant purchases, behaved with uncharacteristic spontaneity, and had so worried her family that she had been sent to the hospital.

Her stay there had not been long. The hospital staff had the wisdom simply to let her alone, and with a minimum of treatment she soon returned to "normal" (that is, her more socially acceptable depression) and was discharged. Since then she had worked at her job faithfully but without much zest, just going through the motions of life.

The picture on the surface seemed doubtful. Her depression was intense, and some previous psychotherapy had not served to prevent her hospitalization. Her behavior made one suspect a manic depressive psychosis, which would be difficult to change. But I had a positive feeling about Doris; something told me she could be helped. There were also some concrete facts which indicated that the situation was not as hopeless as it appeared to be. For one thing, she had come to me, a complete stranger, of her own accord. Then too, I discovered that shortly before her hospitalization she had lost through death her two closest friends, the only two people aside from her immediate family with whom she was positively related. Furthermore, after carefully quizzing her, I did not feel there had ever been a real break with reality. She had always been aware of what she was doing, only she had been powerless to stop herself. Her only "delusion" had been a fixed idea of a man who was dying and rising again. This wasn't really a delusion, however, for she knew all the time that it was an idea of her mind and not an external reality. She seemed greatly relieved when I suggested that her "delusion" gave me confidence: it meant an inner striving for rebirth. I could not at this time go into psychological technicalities, but I did point out the obvious parallel to the death and resurrection of Christ. Hitherto she had just thought of this fixed idea as part of her sickness; the thought that it might be part of her health instead, and even connect her to God, was a new and hopeful idea.

With this feeling that there was something positive at work in Doris I phoned a psychiatrist who knew her. With his recommendation that we undertake counseling (it was his feeling that only good could come out of any constructive human relationship), we agreed to repeat our interviews each week. The counseling was slow work at first as the unconscious was blocked. She was so afraid of it, so deeply distrusting it with its tremendous power to suddenly take over, that dreams were sparse.

However, as she spoke of her past life, and of her present frustrations, there was plenty of material, and the general picture of a bitter conflict of opposites soon emerged. She had complained of a lack of energy and interest in life and of continual depression. But this did not mean there was no psychic activity going on. To the contrary, her inner life was filled with activity and she was aware of its contents. There were always two points of view about everything and she got caught in between them. She had no energy because this conflict of opposites took it all away from her. If we have two horses hitched to our cart, but they are pulling in opposite directions, then we don't get anywhere!

The one point of view expressed conventional attitudes and opinions about what she should do and be like. The other point of view expressed rebellion and resentment. She was naturally afraid of this second point of view. If it took over control of her ego she might again be sent to the hospital. But she couldn't repress it completely. It made its presence felt in countless details of her life and through objectionable thoughts she could not repress. Consequently almost everything she said or did was a matter of conflict. If someone said something to her, the two opposing points of view would debate on its meaning. If she tried to do something, the two points of view would argue over its value.

The conventional opinion, with its awful assortment of Thou-shalts and Thou-shalt-nots, we came to call "the tiger," [1] because every time she gave in to this side of herself it was like feeding a tiger. For the time being the tiger was satisfied, but he soon became hungry again and demanded another meal! The other point of view she felt was more like the devil. It wanted to get her into trouble, to make her say unpleasant things, cause her to feel resentful, and in general to create a rebellion.

It was a surprise to her when I remarked that this devil might in a strange way be in the service of God. For by rebelling he was trying to break through the conventional thinking which gripped her soul and release her to be herself. He was the devil only if she had no connection with him and was overwhelmed involuntarily. But if she could establish a conscious relationship with him, then he could become a creative energy for the transformation of her personality. I was reminded of Nikos Kazantsakis' words about God and the devil. "Someone came. Surely it was God, God . . . or was it the devil? Who can tell them apart? They exchange faces; God sometimes becomes all darkness, the devil all light, and the mind of man is left in a muddle." [2]

It was now clear why she was depressed. With a tiger on the one side and a devil on the other all her inner energy was taken up in conflict and self-reproach. We can regard a depression as a loss of psychic energy by consciousness. When we have psychic energy at our conscious disposal, flowing up from unconscious sources and out into creative expression, then we are happy. When we lose contact with this energy, then we are depressed. But all depressions have within them the seeds of a new creative expression. The energy which has become unconscious is latent and active, and creates new possibilities for the personality if contact with the unconscious inner world can be established.

[157]

From the clinical side it is worth noting that Doris readily understood these inner adversaries as parts of herself. There was never any question of their being "outside of her" or "voices from without." My original feeling that Doris had never truly been psychotic was reinforced by subsequent counseling. In fact, and this is why I tell her story in such detail, her particular conflict was only an exaggeration of a similar conflict which rages inside of every human being in our present culture! Her story is not unusual; it is typical.

An example of her conflict comes from her visits home. Her parents were growing old, and as the only unmarried child she felt a responsibility for their welfare. So in spite of the fact that a visit home was often boring she tried to be the "good daughter" and visit them regularly. She very much wanted to be kind, to make them happy, to help in many little ways. Here, for once, the tiger which told her she should do this united with some positive feeling in herself. But no sooner was she home than the devil asserted himself, and she found herself wrestling with the desire to say the most cutting things, and to express the most negative thoughts. Her very words seemed to have a power of their own, and her thoughts seemed to be not her own but to come involuntarily.

This, by the way, is a good example of how the animus works in a woman. It is he who thinks these independent thoughts and speaks these unexpected words. For this reason many women have the experience of starting with the conscious intention of saying a certain thing and then finding "someone else" speaking through them! This is not abnormal psychology, but it is the way in which the masculine part of a woman's psyche emerges. Lest the male reader become smug about his superiority in this regard, let me remind him of the corresponding lack of control he has over his moods. For the man's anima can seize his moods with just as much force. Quite without his having anything to do about it consciously, the man is in a blue, irritable or resentful mood. Then all his fine masculine thinking degenerates into just so much womanish emotionality! He has been "bewitched." But not knowing he has an anima he will usually blame his poor wife for all his woes!

At any rate, a visit home becomes for Doris a great conflict. If she has succeeded in suppressing the devil she returns exhausted; if she hasn't she returns exhausted and guilty, as the tiger blames her for the things she said. To give another example: at her work her boss takes advantage of her willingness to work hard and overloads her. Naturally the tiger will not let her speak up for herself, so she goes on accepting this as long as possible until eventually the devil becomes overwhelming. Now she is so filled with resentment that she can hardly stand to go to work. A man can detach himself from his boss, be angry at him, and say "to hell with him." But not a woman. She must have some kind of personal relationship to him, and if she feels she is just being used as a thing the situation becomes unbearable for her. In his resentment the devil had a lot of truth on his side. So at long last, she spoke to her boss and expressed some of her resentment over being overloaded. He understood her and took some steps to correct the situation. But poor Doris succumbed now to the tiger and experienced tremendous guilt because she had voiced her negative thoughts!

How had the situation reached such an impasse? It wasn't hard to see as soon as something of her childhood became known. To give just one example: she was raised in a very "Christian" home, meaning a typically moralistic home of the early 20th century. I don't mean it was the worst of all possible homes or that her parents were beasts. Her parents had virtues as well as faults. But they were totally unaware what the soul is like. Possessed by their own unconsciousness, they perpetrated horrible cruelties in the name of Christ. One day the little girl gave way to a sexual curiosity quite common for children. The punishment: for five days no one spoke a word to her. Such things have an almost demonic effect upon a small child, far, far worse than the open fury of the parents which makes them grab the whip. If this is done, at least the child no longer has to feel guilty and the parent no longer has to feel angry! But imagine the amount of guilt, self-reproach, frustrated yearnings for love, and smouldering rebellion which can build up in a sensitive little girl during such a five-day period of isolation. It is in exactly such ways that parts of the personality and emotional life become split off from the main stream of our development and live on in the unconscious, where they wander their own ways, feeling their own emotions, often causing havoc, waiting to be recognized and brought to consciousness in order to become redeemed.

How does a priest or counselor act in such a case? I knew that three things were important, but one above all: the relationship which might spring up between us. In a case like this, the self-reproach is so great that the counselee cannot accept herself without the help of another human being, who sees the darkness of her thoughts as well as she does and yet himself accepts them. Only then can the healing work begin. To create this atmosphere of acceptance may require from the counselor great patience and much careful, attentive listening, for the counselee will let out just a little information at a time to see how it is accepted before divulging more. All this requires a great love for the soul. The priest or minister who gives a quick sermon, a bit of hurried advice, or a nice prayer, does not know what he is doing: he is rejecting the human soul and the God who loves it. The only way such a soul can be reclaimed is through the patience of the counselor, who opens the way for the healing, which comes from God.

Secondly, wherever possible the "tiger" must be weakened. This "tiger" is partly what Freud called the "super-ego". He corresponds to Jung's collective thinking, for his opinions express the collective morality standing in judgment on the personality, plus a host of opinions she held of what she "should" be like derived from the moralistic attitude of parents, church, and society. This is the really negative power, and the rebelliousness is the potentially creative one. So wherever possible these collective opinions must be challenged and corrected with the help of the counselor. It was quite a surprise to Doris when she saw that someone who was a priest, and so stood for God in her mind, did not at all agree with the moral commandments she kept trying to fulfill. This made it possible for her to begin formulating her own moral code and let the tiger starve himself to death.

Thirdly, I felt that the rebellious devil should be listened to. It is interesting that such a rebellious side usually speaks the truth. The thoughts he wants to voice are basically true ones which want to break right through the conventional façade of life to expose the bare truth about people and situations. But he can't be allowed to take total possession of the personality. If he suddenly erupts and overwhelms the ego, which alone has the power of discrimination, he will be most destructive. So Doris, having been instructed and encouraged to listen to what the devil had to say, learned to give also the devil his share, consciously and deliberately and at the proper time. In this way her ego was built up and strengthened and the rebel within her was satisfied.

After several months Doris showed signs of improvement. Her depression lifted, she had more energy, and her relationships with people became more full and confident. The tiger and the devil seemed to have less energy and less power over her strengthened ego. At this point her development reached a new stage. The original opposites, "this is what I ought to do" and "this is what my rebelliousness wants me to do," were somewhat the result of her personal life. Now the conflict between these opponents within her changed into a less dangerous but more basic tension between the two poles of life, between true concern for others and the wish to fulfill her own personal needs; between desires for personal relationship (eros) and the need for a growing consciousness (logos), between yearning to continue her psychological and spiritual progress, opposed by a psychological inertia. Her personal, inner conflict, which was caused largely by her individual life circumstances, was giving way to the general conflict of opposites common to our whole culture. Around the resolution of this conflict swirls all human endeavor; it lives in every man, and it reveals itself eventually in every psychotherapeutic situation and in every dream series.

This problem of the opposites is the point which Doris has reached. Her dreams are concerned with this very problem. This does not surprise us. Since we are generally unaware of the depth of the split in ourselves and do not know of any rational solution, it remains for our inner sagacity to work out an answer.

2

Like an oriental artist who seeks to create a painting with a few bold strokes of his brush, I will try to sketch the problem of the opposites with a few words. Though I will leave much unsaid, I hope that the reader will see the manner in which our Judaeo-Christian heritage has tried to deal with this problem, and how it has failed to solve it.

The problem of the opposites in the Bible begins as soon as man makes his appearance. First it is suggested in the contrast between the two creation stories. The first creation story describes man as made in the image of God. "Then God said, 'Let us make man in our image, after our likeness. . . . So God created man in his own image, in the image of God he created him." [3] But the second creation story says: ". . . then the Lord God formed man of dust from the ground. . . ." [4] This is not a contradiction but a paradox. Man is torn between his divine image and his lowly earthy substance.

The story of the origin of the opposites is told even more graphically in the second creation story's tale of the first man and the first woman. Adam and Eve live in innocent bliss in the beautiful Paradise of Eden. Everything is permitted them, save one thing: they must not eat of the tree of the knowledge of good and evil. Unfortunately there is one flaw in the garden of Eden—the snake. It tempts Eve, appealing to her desire for power and knowledge, "to be like God, knowing good and evil," [5] and she in turn tempts Adam. Man and woman eat the forbidden fruit. As they do so their eyes are opened, they experience shame, and in the realization of their opposite sexuality, they make themselves aprons of fig leaves. Their bliss is shattered because now they know the opposites. With this knowledge, guilt, shame and fear have entered into human existence. Now as they hear the Lord approaching they hide, but to no avail. He calls them, and Adam answers, " 'I heard the sound of thee in the garden, and I was afraid, because I was naked; and I hid myself.' He said, 'Who told you that you were naked?' " [6] To be told something is to become aware of something we did not know before. Now Adam and Eve know.

However else we may take this story it certainly is a story with profound psychological meaning. It tells us that man's original innocent harmony with creation is shattered the moment moral consciousness dawns upon him. For with the dawn of moral consciousness his natural wholeness falls apart into two seemingly hostile halves. This produces in man guilt and fear, and the burden of moral consciousness expressed in the sentence from God to toil and suffer in exile from Paradise. The beast of prey in the jungle knows no guilt, but lives according to its nature without thinking about it. Were it to receive the gift of self-awareness, and the knowledge of good and evil, its paradisiacal wholeness would also be shattered.

I cannot resist at this point commenting upon the presence of the serpent in the garden. The traditional ecclesiastical teaching that God is the *summum bonum* ascribes all evil to man and all goodness to God. It was thus man's evil, his weakness, which introduced sin into the world. Man alone is the guilty one, and God has no part in his fall. Unfortunately, however, this ancient story from Genesis hints at God's own involvement in human tragedy. After all, who brought the serpent into Paradise? Was it not God? Who created Adam and Eve with their curiosity to be "like God," and their desire to *know*, so that they would respond to the tempting voice of the serpent? Should not we suspect that the whole drama was a carefully staged plot by God, who wanted His creature man to be a supremely moral being, not a blissful idiot? For God must have known that the only road to moral value leads through pain and suffering and that the confrontation of opposites is unavoidable.

In talking of God's plot, His responsibility, and so forth, I am of course talking of God as man sees Him. I do not mean to ascribe to Him an anthropomorphic character. How God is in Himself is not for man to know. We only know Him as he manifests Himself in creation, in the Bible, and in the psyche. It is God as He appears to us to be that we are here concerned with. We are almost forced to use anthropomorphic language to describe this image of God we hold in our minds. But it would be naïve to think that such language can actually describe Him in His essence. This essence of God is beyond our rational comprehension, at least in this life.

Leaving aside these questions for the moment, it is surprising to find that the Bible begins with the split nature of man. The rest of the Bible can be viewed as the story of man's growing awareness of what he felt God was doing to recreate man's wholeness on a higher level. This re-creation is to take place not on the level of Eden's Paradise (an angel with a flaming sword forbids man's return), but on a higher level of consciousness. How will this solution be worked out? Will the dark earth side of man with its devilish curiosity be driven from the face of the earth to leave man in pure goodness? Or will there occur a reconciliation of the opposites, a unique realization of man's total nature?

At first the conflict between the opposites only deepens. Adam and Eve conceive children, but alas, the children reflect the opposition in man more strongly than ever! Cain and Abel are incompatible. Cain, who represents evil, kills Abel, who stands for good. God accepts sacrifices of Abel instead of Cain, whom He banishes but does not kill; this throws a glaring light upon the conflict of the opposites, since Cain still seems to be necessary. The figure of Cain is of particular significance for the development of human consciousness.

The objections that could be raised to such treatment of the Bible come from two different camps. Those who accept the Bible as an historic document might object to my point of view as being too psychological. But an attempt to understand the psychological meaning of the Biblical stories does not say anything against the historical value of these stories. Whether or not Adam and Eve lived as actual people, the story is still filled with important truth about the development of man and his understanding of God. It is this truth and not Biblical criticism that we are concerned with.

Others, who do not believe in the Bible, will perhaps ask why one should believe that Cain, Abel or the other Biblical figures ever existed? Such a question is psychologically naïve. Cain and Abel might never have lived, Jeremiah might be a fiction, the gospel records may be totally untrustworthy from an historical viewpoint—the fact nevertheless remains that the Bible was recorded because it reflects the story of man's growing awareness of himself and of God, and this alone matters at this point.

The second attempt at a solution of the problem of the opposites comes in the story of Noah's ark, a story which —according to scholars—has its antecedents in Babylonian lore. In this story the attempt is made to select the good men and destroy the rest; perhaps in this way wickedness will be stamped out of man, and he can become "perfect" by becoming pure. So the flood comes and everyone is destroyed except the good Noah and his family. The only effect, however, is a change in the image of God as man sees Him, man remains the same and continues to be partly evil, for shortly after the flood, Noah becomes drunk with wine, his youngest son mocks him, and in return Noah places a curse upon him. Hardly an auspicious beginning for the remaining "good" men of the earth!

Man is not changed by the flood, but his understanding is! From now on God is described as growing in self-awareness. He recognizes the inescapable reality of evil in His creature, man. As long as man is man, evil will be with him. So the Lord says, "I will never again curse the ground because of man, for the imagination of man's heart is evil from his youth; neither will I ever again destroy every living creature as I have done." [7]

There is one further attempt in the Book of Genesis to solve the problem of opposites, but it has gone largely unnoticed. We have already mentioned it. It is the story of Jacob's struggle with his adversary. Here a solution was hinted at: if man will only wrestle consciously with the adversary in himself he will be blessed, for he will be wrestling with God.

When the Book of Genesis failed to solve the problem of the opposites, another attempt at a solution was made in the Book of Exodus, in the form of the law. The law is the whole body of moral and religious legislation which according to the Bible began with the tribal laws under Moses and ended with the complex legislation of the priests. Never has the world seen such an extensive body of rules and moral aids for every act and thought in life. The solution these laws offer to the problem of the opposites is this: we will lay down rules and laws for man to follow; if man follows them, then God will be with him and man will prosper. If he does not, then God may forsake him. This amounted to an agreement between God and man. This agreement is the Covenant or Testament from which the Old Testament gets its name. As Moses puts it, "If you will diligently hearken to the voice of the Lord your God, and do that which is right in his eyes, and give heed to his commandments and keep all his statutes, I will put none of the diseases upon you which I put upon the Egyptians, for I am the Lord, your healer." [8]

The idea was to give man a definite plan and rule for his life; by his following them, evil would become powerless. But alas! the difficulty was that man could not fulfill the law, just because he also had evil in him. In spite of his best conscious intentions and efforts he kept slipping. And always just around the corner was the old guilt and fear, the old realization that he was not yet whole but torn asunder.

Nevertheless, the men of the Old Testament tried to make the Old Covenant or law work. Perhaps, the prophets thought, if men will only become aware of the extent to which they are flaunting the law they will exert greater efforts and accomplish the task. So began the period of the great prophets. Men like Amos and Jeremiah and Hosea and a host of others harangued and exhorted and implored man to follow the law, do away with idolatrous worship of voluptuous foreign gods and obey the Lord. In the process they immeasurably increased Israel's awareness of God. The old nationalistic Jahweh became a God for all the world, and the localized God of Mt. Sinai became the Creator of all the universe. They also sharpened man's moral consciousness and forged that sharp sword, the Judaeo-Christian conscience, which has so influenced our world.

But with all this great emphasis upon God's demands for justice, correct worship, and charitable deeds, the cleavage in man between what seemed to him good and evil only deepened. (I say "what seemed" to him good and evil since we do not know what good and evil might be in an absolute sense any more than we know God in an absolute sense. We only know what seems to us to be good and evil from our human point of view, just as we can only comprehend God through an image or understanding of Him in our minds). Indeed, the situation became well-nigh desperate, for black seems all the darker when contrasted with white. Preach what they might, the prophets were unable to exhort men to sufficient goodness.

But while in one way the prophets' increased moral emphasis served to deepen the cleavage in men, in another way it promoted the conditions necessary for the resolution of the problem. For the problem of opposites has to be clearly seen before it can be solved. The prophets helped towards a clarification, but they could not supply the final answer. No matter how a man tried to banish his anger, desire, passion, and self-seeking, the old problem, the dark drives, remained.

Obviously the situation required something new. And slowly there came the realization that the answer could not come from man, but God Himself would have to do something. So there arose, in the latter part of the Old Testament, the longing for a Messiah. It was expected that God Himself would send someone who would set things right upon earth!

There is no systematic thinking in the Old Testament about the Messiah. The passages which speak of him are born out of the passion of a people undergoing great suffering, not from rational thought processes. But generally the teaching was that God would raise up for Himself a special emissary, a saviour, who would stamp out evil and forge a new kingdom of justice and goodness upon the earth. Jeremiah writes: "Behold, the days are coming, says the Lord, when I will raise up for David a righteous Branch, and he shall reign as king, and deal wisely, and execute justice and righteousness in the land. In his days Judah will be saved, and Israel will dwell securely." [9] The coming of the Messiah would usher in the "Day of the Lord"; this would be the creation of a new and just world, and the destruction of the old evil and injustice. Therefore it was a day to be feared as well as longed for: "Let all the inhabitants of the land tremble, for the day of the Lord is coming, it is near, a day of darkness and gloom, a day of clouds and thick darkness!" [10]

What the law could not accomplish was now expected from God. The hope that He would directly intervene in human affairs was a new step towards the solution of the problem, for it meant that it was no longer just up to man; God also would do something about it. But the means the Messiah would employ were not original. We see again the old answer: destroy the evil, solidify the good, solve the problem of opposites by eliminating one of them.

Only one prophet had an intimation that the Messiah might be different from what was anticipated. Isaiah thought of the Messiah in a strangely paradoxical way. He would come, not as the champion of the good over the evil, but as a paradoxical saviour, who would save men by his own moral suffering. "He was despised and rejected by men; a man of sorrows and acquainted with grief; and as one from whom men hide their faces he was despised, and we esteemed him not." [11]

So man looked forward to a new answer to his problem,

this time from God and not from man. This new answer the Christians saw in the birth of God as a man in the person of Jesus Christ. To solve man's problem, God Himself became a man. In Jesus Christ the living God and earthly man were united.

The Christian teaching contains the possibility of a new kind of psychological development in man. The statement "God preferred to become a man" not only says something about God, but also something about man. For now that God Himself had become man, man has the possibility for understanding his nature in a new way. The teaching about God having become man represents the possibility for the achievement of psychological wholeness. Until now man had tried to stand whole before God by his own moral efforts and he failed. Now that God Himself had become man, human nature had a renewed hope for a wholeness which God would make possible.

To suggest that Christian theological statements also have psychological implications is not to negate or devalue theology, nor do I mean to say that theology is nothing but psychology. Properly regarded, theological statements are concerned with a metaphysical realm of reality not ordinarily perceivable by man. In this realm the Christian theology has a complex and manifold meaning which is not under discussion here. Just the same, there is a correspondence between the metaphysical realm and the realm within man. Christian theology is not isolated from man's experience but deeply concerned with it. Corresponding psychic realities and possibilities do exist within man. Christian theology contributes to the solution of man's problem of opposites on a psychological, experimental level. This is what we are here concerned with.

To the psychological problem of opposites, God in

[*171*]

Christ answers (I speak of course figuratively): "When I am fully expressed in your life, then will the totality of your own nature be expressed, since I Myself have chosen your human nature. When your own totality is thus expressed, then the conflict of your opposites will have ceased, and will have been replaced by the harmony which is at the heart of My universe." But when God has expressed Himself in man, then man has also expressed his own nature completely. Or, put another way: when man has expressed his own totality, then he has given expression to his Creator. This is how close the relationship is between God and our total self.

The tension between the new understanding of the relationship of God and man which Christ brought and the old understanding of Judaism was naturally great. The old form and the new form had moved so far apart that those Jews who accepted the new expression of Judaism in Christ eventually were alienated from their fellows. What began as the fulfillment of Judaism came to stand alone, separated from its honored parent.

Every new breakthrough into consciousness has to struggle against opposition from human egocentricity and conventionality. Such was the case with the radical answer God gave to the problem of opposites. "Bring to birth the whole man." At the birth of the infant Jesus, Herod, who represented literally and symbolically all entrenched human egocentricity, for he feared the "new king" would replace him, sought violently to destroy the child. Only the intervention of divine forces through dreams prevented the untimely destruction of the new birth in man. Again at the inception of His ministry, Christ had to struggle against terrible forces which would have blocked His way. First Satan rose up; "Use your power to feed mankind," said

Satan, that is to satisfy what human beings think they need, food, instead of what they really need, wholeness. "Use your power to rule over the cities of the world," said Satan another time. That is, forego the kingdom of the soul for a tangible, earthly realm. "Use your power for self-glorification," said Satan a third time. That is, use the powers of the total man to glorify the ego instead of God. We may take this story as a fully credible authentic account of the inner struggle Jesus must have gone through when He realized the enormity of His task, and of the great danger to the ego of inflation whenever it approaches the powers of the center. Only consciousness of one's ego motives avails at such a time. But He also had to struggle against the traditional collective values enshrined in the family life of His time. He puts the case as sharply as possible: "If anyone comes to me and does not hate his own father and mother and wife and children and brothers and sisters, yes, and even his own life, he cannot be my disciple." [12] And in many places we read how Jesus rejects too tight bonds of family. "Behold, his mother and his brothers stood outside, asking to speak to him. But he replied to the man who told him, 'Who is my mother, and who are my brothers?' And stretching out his hand toward his disciples, he said, 'Here are my mother and my brothers! For whoever does the will of my Father in heaven is my brother, and sister, and mother.' " [13] What was taking place within Christ was so new that it could only be accomplished by a violent breaking away from the collective values of the past, which, however valuable they might be, always are too traditional to be the medium for new expressions of God. [14]

But how can the complexity of human nature be expressed as the whole, therefore Christlike, man? How can irreconcilable opposites be expressed in one life? Only

[*173*]

through a highly paradoxical center of reconciliation, a secret known only to God, which can only be accomplished through the intervention of God. The first Christians said God chose to be born through Mary, by the intervention of the Holy Spirit, since they knew human agency alone could not bring the miracle about. Man's limited and rational consciousness could not conceive of an answer to the problem of opposites.

Christ's life could only end upon the Cross. Men were not yet ready to accept such a radical solution as that which God offered. So Christ had to be crucified on a Cross. The outstretched arms of this Cross express symbolically the opposites which unite at the center. The four-armed Cross is an example of a mandala, a design or symbol expressing totality through a circle or square. But unlike Eastern mandalas, which are more abstract designs, the Christian symbol is rooted in the earth. For Christianity emphasizes that the totality of the psyche is to be accomplished in this earthly life and not by release from it into "heaven." Christ was crucified between two thieves, the one who repented and the other who did not; heaven and hell, the motif of the opposites thus being carried out to the bitter end.[15]

Those who crucified Him were not murderers or thieves, the usual "sinners." He was killed because men could not tolerate His demands for consciousness. His Crucifixion was sought by men who were the best religious leaders of the time, who could not tolerate Him because the new message He embodied would completely upset the traditional and collective religious conceptions. Men have always violently resisted changes which would force them into a new consciousness. Christ was such a change.

He came too early even for His Jewish disciples. Only a

[*174*]

few understood what had really happened through Christ. They too deserted Him at first.

But what had happened through Christ could not be destroyed that easily. What God had done men could not undo. So the death on the Cross was followed by the Resurrection. The irrationality of the answer of God triumphed over the rationality of men. Speaking psychologically, the reconciling center in man continued to live and offer men hope. For it enabled men to grasp the miracle of the resurrected Christ and to become aware of the possibility for their own wholeness which they could not reach under the law. Even today, when our ego consciousness "dies with Christ" as we realize the conflicts of our nature and become impaled on the Cross of the opposites, we "rise with Him" again through a new relationship to our center.

In Christ the warring opposites had been united in a paradoxical unity wrought by God. Naturally such a solution escaped man's rational intellect and refused to be cast into conceptual forms. For this reason all theories of the atonement eventually run into one objection or another.

The Incarnation and the Crucifixion of Christ do not permit any logically consistent theory as to their meaning, yet they still have a profound effect upon men. The best example we have from early Christian literature of the impact of Christ on one of His Jewish brethren is the story of the former Pharisee Saul of Tarsus, the later St. Paul. Here we have the reconciling nature of Christ in all of its naked paradox. St. Paul felt himself torn between the opposites. He writes to the Romans:

> I do not understand my own actions. For I do not do what I want but I do the very thing I hate. . . . So then it is no longer I that do it, but sin which dwells within me. . . . I

can will what is right, but I cannot do it. For I do not do the good I want, but the evil I do not want is what I do. . . . So I find it to be a law that when I want to do right, evil lies close at hand. . . . Wretched man that I am! Who will deliver me from this body of death? [16]

These are the words of a man of sensitive conscience who recognizes his human dilemma. He sees the apparently irreconcilable opposites which war in him against his will. His reaction cannot be explained rationally, for it is based upon an irrational experience; "Thanks be to God through Jesus Christ our Lord!" Christ has saved him from his dilemma through a mystery which cannot be explained with words.

The result is a fundamental transformation of Paul. Gone is the old man with his narrow ego-consciousness. Paul has been baptized with Christ, buried with Him, and trans-formed through Him into newness of life.[17] The result is that Paul's psychic life no longer is centered in the ego, but in what would correspond psychologically to the self. "I have been crucified with Christ [impaled on the opposites]; it is no longer I who live, but Christ who lives in me." [18]

Theologically Paul knew Christ as the Incarnation of God. Psychologically he knew Christ as a living force within himself, reconciling Paul to himself. The theological formulation and the inner, psychological experience do not cancel each other out, they belong together.

But what has happened today to this Christian answer to man's psychological dilemma? Any pastoral counselor or psychotherapist knows that in spite of the Cross many people do not feel or act redeemed. The old conflict rages on unconsciously in all of us. And anyone who looks at our world will see it is an unredeemed world, in which the warring opposites confront us on every side. Why do we

[176]

Christians talk about redemption through Christ while so many of us do not feel redeemed?

From the point of view of psychology, this was unavoidable because the usual Christian's understanding of Christ leaves out the dark side of man from our relationship to God. Instead of a reconciliation of opposites taking place, and a wholeness emerging, a one-sidely "perfect" man is held up to the Christian as the conscious goal of his religious life. But this leaves the unredeemed shadow side of man in a chaotic condition, banished to the unconscious psychic realm, from which position he perpetuates the war of the opposites. We can rightly assert that we are not yet redeemed in a psychological sense.

Psychologically, the coming of Christ into history coincides with the emergence of a reconciling center in man capable of uniting the opposites one to another in a paradoxical unity which can restore man's wholeness. The salvation which Christ makes possible in a theological, historical sense has its psychological parallel in a Christlike center in man which when experienced—as with Paul—results in a release from guilt, a restoration of inner harmony, and a feeling of oneness with God. But the tension of this paradox was more than men could hold at that time. Specifically, man could not tolerate the inclusion of man's morally ambiguous side into the picture of human totality, and he could not accept the irrational solution of the conflict of opposites as implied by Christ the God-man and Reconciler. As a result the psychological wholeness was not fully realized, and the conflict of opposites continued. A glance at later Christian development will illustrate this.

We can see the failure to resolve the split of human nature even within the pages of the New Testament, for in the later epistles of the New Testament the conflict of the

[*177*]

opposites again becomes manifest. The Epistles of John and
of Peter are filled with admonitions like "eschew evil, and
do good." [19] The author of I John writes: "If we say that
we have no sin, we deceive ourselves, and the truth is not in
us. If we confess our sins, he is faithful and just, and will
forgive our sins and cleanse us from all unrighteousness." [20]
Notice the "cleanse us": we are to be cleansed of evil, so
that it no longer exists. But alas! Now the poor Christian is
back where he started. For he soon realizes that shortly
after being "cleansed" his evil starts to appear again! That
dark spot in him just won't wash away.

So the conflict resumes all the more bitterly. Once again
there is the desperate struggle to eliminate the dark oppo-
nent. Finally this reaches an extremity in the Book of Revelation. Here Christ is confronted by Satan or the Anti-
Christ, and a fearful battle rages. In this struggle Christ is
no longer a saving, forgiving figure, but a ruthless avenger
of evil:

> Then I saw heaven opened, and behold, a white horse! He
> who sat upon it is called Faithful and True, and in right-
> eousness he judges and makes war. His eyes are like a flame
> of fire, and on his head are many diadems; and he has a name
> inscribed which no one knows but himself. He is clad in a
> robe dipped in blood, and the name by which he is called is
> The Word of God. And the armies of heaven, arrayed in
> fine linen, white and pure, followed him on white horses.
> From his mouth issues a sharp sword with which to smite
> the nations, and he will rule them with a rod of iron; he will
> tread the wine press of the fury of the wrath of God the
> Almighty.[21]

The saving figure of Christ on the Cross has become the
figure of a relentless judge, identified with good, warring
against evil. In his "righteousness" he has turned into an

angry executor. We see how overemphasis of one side always leads to disaster. The net result for man is of course most unfortunate. Only 144,000 are saved and the rest are damned, "and if any one's name was not found in the book of life, he was thrown into the lake of fire." [22]

It does not take much imagination to perceive that the war of the opposites had resumed in the Christian tradition as intensely as before. Many a Christian saw himself more in danger of damnation than ever, and his Saviour had turned into his judge.

The debates in the early Church over the meaning of the humanity of Christ also illustrate the declining awareness of the paradox of the reconciliation of opposites. If we look at the life of Christ as it is given us in the Synoptics we get the impression of a very whole human being. Now of course we cannot prove how reliable the Gospels are as historical documents, and strictly speaking we cannot say or know for sure what the "historical Jesus" was like. Nevertheless, we do have the Gospel records, and at the least we can say this is the impression some people received. We can note the following facts: the Christ was born of a simple peasant girl in a stable. Like any man He was subject to temptation, which is why He had to wrestle against Satan. He could become angry, He became inflamed at the hypocrites among the scribes and Pharisees, He agressively drove out the money-changers, He could lose heart and had to make an effort to overcome his own fear in the garden of Gethsemane. He ate, drank, associated with sinners, and was called a "glutton and a drunkard." [23] In short, His humanity was as complete and as real as our humanity.

This completeness of Christ's human nature was first defended, then obscured and forgotten in the teaching of the early Church. Originally the Fathers fought a noble war against heresies which would have destroyed the essence of the Christian message of the God-man, for instance against the Gnostics, who acknowledged the reality of both spirit and matter, but believed they were entirely separate principles which could have nothing to do with each other. According to the Gnostics, man in his sensual, earthly, material nature belonged to the world of evil. Therefore it was unthinkable that God could really have become human. This led to the Gnostic doctrine of Docetism (a word which comes from the Greek *dokein* meaning "to seem"), which taught that Christ only seemed to be human. He was just acting out the role of man, acting as though He suffered and died; but in reality He was God and not man, and therefore could not be subject to human, material imperfection. With gallantry the Church rejected this high-sounding heresy and clung to its paradox: that in Christ God and man, the spiritual and the physical, were united.

On the other hand were those known as adoptionists, who taught the deceptively simple doctrine that Jesus was only a unique man, filled with the power of God, one with God by virtue of his love to Him, but not identical in substance with God. Thus Christ according to this teaching was essentially just a man, just as in Gnostic teaching He was essentially God. A teaching such as this had the virtue of a simplicity not found in such catholic creedal formulations as the Nicene Creed. It might easily have won the day. But from the psychological, as well as from the theological, point of view this would have been a disaster, for it would have missed the mystery of the whole man: that in the fulness of life the transcendental as well as the human is expressed. So it is fortunate that after a struggle this heresy was also rejected by the Church. It is highly impressive to see with what tenacity and brilliance the Fathers defended

[*180*]

and preserved the essentials of a Christology which has the psychological merit of reflecting the paradoxical wholeness of man.

Unfortunately, however, as time went on the Church could not hold the tension of this paradox. The Fathers wanted to keep the doctrine that Christ was God and man, yet they could not bear the idea that human imperfection could have been in Him. So the human Christ who shows through the Gospel narratives became obscured and increasingly identified with a one-sided righteousness. He became good, brilliantly perfect man, without spot of sin; naturally by comparison actual human beings looked all the blacker and more evil. Because of this, man's shadowy, and especially his instinctual, earthly nature was once more excluded from a relationship to God, and so fell prey psychologically to those very errors of Gnosticism which they had refuted theologically. Those emotions and desires which are rooted in the body and are produced or accompanied by chemical changes in the body were particularly excluded from the kind of humanity the Church held up before their people as the Christian goal. This included anger, passion, earthly love, sexual desire, and so forth. Man's spirit, but not his body, was brought into relationship with God.[24]

We can partly understand this difficulty in dealing with man's physical nature from the spirit of the times. Christianity was born in an extremely sensual era, and man's precariously won Christian conscience and spiritual outlook could all too easily have been overwhelmed by the predominant instinctuality of the times. The early Church was able to save man's spirit only by rejecting his body and did not see the possibility for a reconciliation of the two. For this reason, the writings of the Fathers, brilliant

[*181*]

though they are, lack the same feeling of wholeness and human warmth which we gain from the picture of Jesus in the Gospels.

It would be interesting to trace the Church's teaching about Christ, His humanity, and the nature of His salvation throughout the centuries. We would certainly see that in the Middle Ages the Church tended to fall once more into a teaching of salvation by a kind of law, that is by prescribing specific actions and sacraments which would eliminate evil from man. Later, during the Reformation, Martin Luther sought to revive the older Pauline experience with Christ as a reconciling center within himself. But soon this solution fell away into Puritanism's and Calvinism's rigid morality, and an even more violent opposition within man took place.

What is the outcome of this ancient struggle between the opposites in man? One glance at our world tells us that men are not whole, and one look into the unconscious depth of almost any one of us shows that the struggle of the opposites continues. The Incarnation and the Cross, like "highly polished stones"—to use a simile originated by Dr. Jung— are still regarded with reverent awe. But because we have lost contact with the corresponding, reconciling symbols in the unconscious, our reverent contemplation seldom moves the inner life. The Christian tree is uprooted and preserved in a glass freezer. We gaze at its cold beauty but cannot touch its living essence, because its roots are no longer in the soil of the soul.

It is the religious task of our age to reroot this Christian tree in the living substance of our inner being. Then that symbol which Christ brings to life will become known to us again, and we will become men who know we can hope for wholeness. Our dreams—in strange and wonderful ways—reflect the life process at work in us which seeks to make us aware of this Christlike, reconciling symbol of totality.

3

We are the inheritors of the unresolved conflict of the opposites which I have called the Christian problem. Our entire Christian culture suffers from this problem. Doris first felt it through her parents. In trying to be "Christians" they identified themselves only with what seemed good and moral. In this one-sided identification they lost much that was human in them, and perpetrated psychic cruelties on their sensitive daughter. In the name of righteousness they isolated her from all human contact for five days, driving her into the arms of the devil. As in the case of the Christ of Revelation, judgment replaced love. Doris fell victim to evil, the very thing they tried to eradicate.

Doris confronted the same problem when she sought her own wholeness. Even though she learned to lessen the demands of her collective conscience, and to deal more constructively with her "devil," beneath the surface lurked basic oppositions which could not be handled so easily. These opposites seemed irreconcilable, and yet some reconciliation of the light and dark had to take place within her in order for her to attain the wholeness which she so much desired. The actual, human situation of Doris is directly connected with the religious history which we have discussed.

To see how our dreams are commenting on this problem, we will now look at three dreams of a man who also wrestled heavily with the problem of opposites in himself. Like Doris, he too had a sensitive conscience, he too identified himself exclusively with goodness. Thus he fell victim

[*183*]

to onslaughts from his own unrecognized dark feelings and emotions. The result had been a bitter split in himself, which had finally driven him to study his dreams in an attempt to effect a resolution. He reported his first dream as follows:

> A man about my own age appeared. He was hostile to me, and our encounter led to a violent struggle. After we had wrestled for some time a fiery vehicle descended near us; inside was a man who called to the one with whom I struggled. The man with whom I had been wrestling broke from me and departed with the other man, who was older, in the strange fiery craft. I watched them leave. An unknown companion stood near me and also watched.

The reader will not have much difficulty in recognizing that the dreamer struggles in the dream with his shadow. His "other side" appears as an assailant, an adversary, striving to overcome him. This is so far a familiar motif.

There are, however, two types of shadows. In Tom's case [25] the shadow represented certain qualities in his life which he did not develop or had repressed. This was his personal shadow, with features that originated in Tom's past life. In addition to a personal shadow like this we can distinguish the archetypal shadow, a figure of the collective unconscious. The archetypal shadow need not be concerned with specific details or deeds of our life. He represents the sum total of that part of human nature which the spirit of our times has rejected or ignored. In this case, the shadow did not represent the dreamer's personal, unredeemed past, but the one-sidedness of our present culture, which is unable to successfully integrate the darker, fallible side of human nature, and virtually forces everyone to identify with only one side.

This particular man had tried hard to be a "Christian." In so doing he had identified himself with goodness, kindness, altruism, reasonableness, and calmness. But it is not in human nature to be completely noble and good, just as an apple split in half cannot be called a whole apple. There are opposite tendencies in every man which remain unconscious and form themselves into another man inside of himself. In this case this other man was sensual, self-seeking, not reasonable but irrational, not calm but passionate, not spiritual but material.

How shall we deal with this other, split-off side of ourselves? I must stress that "integrating" the shadow does not mean giving him license. To give license to our lust or cruelty or self-seeking integrates nothing. It only represses our other, positive side. As a matter of fact, it is dangerous to give license to our shadow. But if we are able to become one with our good side, it is possible to reach out a helping hand and integrate our lower nature.

So it is not a matter of either-or, but of both-and. We cannot say, "I will cast aside all my previous moral values and give my shadow license." For traditional morality contains values which also are part of the whole man.

That is why the dreamer has such a fearful struggle. He cannot let his shadow overcome him, for then his ego-consciousness would be eclipsed and he would succumb to his shadow. The one-sidedness would remain, but in a different direction. Instead, the tension between the two must be held until they can reach some accord, and the values of both ego and shadow can become fairly represented in consciousness.

Jung said about our collective shadow that he is 90 per cent pure gold! Without a contact with our shadow we would become self-righteous, devoid of life, lacking in human understanding, sexually cold, unable to have living relationships with people, cut off from the earth, just plain dull, and subject to unconscious cruelties of a frightful proportion. When we look at some of the puritanic Christians who have tried to identify themselves with only righteousness, we can see this amply illustrated. The history of the world abounds with men who identified themselves with the good and the right and perpetrated inhuman horrors. We need to recognize our shadows if we are to become human, flexible, and forgiving, just as the elder son needed to recognize his prodigal brother in the famous parable.

The dreamer's shadow, then, must also play his part, but ego and shadow are so opposed to each other that apparently the matter cannot be resolved, and this is the problem on which the personality is stuck.

But what about the older man who takes the shadow with him in a fiery vehicle? The fiery vehicle reminded the dreamer of the fiery chariot which swept Elijah into the sky, and of the fiery furnace which descended upon Abraham.[26] Fire is emotion and energy par excellence. It represents chemically a transformation of substance, and the release of energy from inert matter in the form of heat and light. In psychology too there is energy, the basic energy of the psyche. The fire of the psyche comes from the biochemical life of the body which in an unknown way is transformed into autonomous spirit or fire. It can be a destructive fire, inflaming the ego into passionate actions, or burning up the ego with energies with which the ego cannot cope. Or it can be a creative fire, providing the ego with the substance and inspiration of creativity, and rising up as a great expression of love.

In the former case it is the fire of the devil, in the latter it

[*186*]

is the fire of the Holy Ghost, for fire is one of the basic Biblical symbols for God. It was through fire that God spoke to Moses, through fire He led the people of Israel, through fire He would purge the earth on the Day of the Lord, through tongues of fire that He inspired the apostles. Psychologically, we know God when we come into creative contact with the fire of basic, psychic energy. If we can sustain this fire we experience the Holy Spirit, if we cannot we are plunged into the flame of hell, for the devil too has his fire.

The man in the vehicle has to do with this fire. He can control it and use it for special purposes. We surmise, then, that he hints at the self, or the total man. It is from this total man that the shadow comes, to engage the dreamer in struggle. Shadow and self are always closely linked, as Jacob discovered in his famous wrestling.

But who is the unknown man who stood silently by the dreamer at the conclusion of the battle? The dreamer scarcely noticed him. The unknown man said nothing. Perhaps he is connected with the figure in the fiery vehicle. The dreamer, because he accepted the struggle, has now an unknown man in himself, a man who is not the ego but beyond the ego. The dream ends on this encouraging note.

But basically the dream shows a bitter conflict of opposites which seems to have little chance of a solution. How can good and evil, egoism and altruism, instinct and disciplined morality, be brought into accord? How do the masculine and the feminine unite into a higher entity? How is the material man to be reconciled with the spiritual man? Small wonder the struggle was so furious and so inconclusive!

The dreamer was a person with insight and saw the meaning and proportions of what was happening. After

[*187*]

some months of diligently seeking a way through these opposites he had the following dream.

> There is a split; Southerners are against Northerners. Contingents from each group go out to meet each other, to confer and negotiate. The Virginians are there; they are exceedingly cruel and carry guns. I wander up to them and mix with them, but we do not fight. Their leader, a son, leads us downward into a huge subterranean area; here they put on a great demonstration, sort of as the hosts of hell. It is like a grand opera in which they sing forth a mighty song and chorus. Their leader looks somewhat like Errol Flynn. They seem to realize their invincible power and inevitable triumph. Then at the end I, also a son, go forward to meet them, silently, somewhat shyly. I show the devil-leader something in my hand, perhaps like a card, in utter simplicity. The countenance of the devil-leader changes startlingly as he reads the unknown card, beginning with a look of *utmost astonishment,* and then registering defeat.

The dreamer had been a student of the Civil War. For him the war meant an implacable split in something essentially one, a split most difficult to heal, and a war of frightful cruelty and horror. Errol Flynn represented for him someone amoral, in stark contrast to his own sophisticated Christian conscience. The dreamer did not know what he held in his hand. He seemed to know what it was in the dream and that it had been given him by someone, but on awakening he could not identify it.

The dream begins by showing the problem of opposites dramatically as a civil war within the personality, a split between Southerners and Northerners. This motif had presented itself in previous dreams, but in this instance the possibility for reconciliation is present, for contingents from each group are beginning to negotiate. That is, each side may be prepared to give a little in order to arrive at an agreement. Now the dreamer himself appears as the leader of the Northern forces; but corresponding to him is a shadow-figure who leads the Southerners. The dreamer was born and raised in the North, but his mother came originally from the South. The South therefore he associated with the "mother country." This suggests a connection between the dreamer's shadow and the "mother world" of love, instinct, and passion. Now, with the appearance of this dark "son," it looks as if things might get out of hand. Like the adversary in the previous dream, he represents all the dreamer's own opposition to morals, his immorality, his devilry, the rebel within him who knows lust and hate and who can do evil. As such he puts on a regular demonstration of the forces of hell. The dream becomes like a great drama of evil foreboding the ultimate victory of darkness within the personality.

But then at the end of the dream, the dreamer goes forward to the "son" of Satan and shows him something in his hand. What this something was the dreamer himself does not know upon awakening, but it provokes the utmost astonishment in the other "son." [27] It is something which suggests utter simplicity, and yet which astonishes the adversary from the unconscious; it brings the recognition of defeat into the eyes of this dark leader of hell. What was the miraculous possession the dreamer held in his hand? Perhaps something which could force the dark forces within him into renewed negotiation, and compel them to give up all further attempts to overcome him. It is something of such a secret and unknown nature that the dreamer himself did not know what he possessed.

Evidently it is not something which just overcomes or eliminates the dark side of the personality. The dreamer is

[*189*]

willing to negotiate with his other side, to recognize that, like the South, it is also part of the Union. Indeed, like the South, this other side cannot be called evil in spite of its devilish aspects. It is simply different from consciousness and at odds with it. So we may take the secret thing the dreamer has as something unknown which may effect a reconciliation with the rebellious forces of the personality. Such a saving symbol is the self, the total man, the paradoxical unity of the whole person.

As yet, however, the exact nature of this unity escapes the dreamer's awareness. He has it, but it is still an unknown, relatively unconscious reality to him. So the inner work goes on for several more months with occasional depressions. Then comes the following astonishing dream:

> Some of us are making a great effort. We are trying again and again to do something. In the early morning I am still working on the project, though my wife is very sleepy. It involves some pieces of metal. There is a feeling of intense discouragement. I am trying to put some things together. At the end, my hand is upon a cube, or almost a cube, of metal, when to my great surprise the metal begins to behave in an unusual manner. It becomes alive, sort of magnetic. It attracts things. I marvel greatly and call my wife. In fact, I am terribly surprised. It is wonderful, but also dreadful. I am filled with surprise, wonder and fear. It is a great and dreadful event.

The feeling of discouragement in the dream reflected the dreamer's actual feelings: in spite of his perseverance his work had as yet little outward signs of success. The metal was not like anything the dreamer could remember from his personal life, except possibly a magnet. This dream had a profound impression upon the dreamer and lifted him out of his depression.

[*190*]

This dream is remarkable because of its similarity to alchemy, which tried to transform base metals into gold or some other refined substance. The end goal of this alchemical process was described as finding the "stone of the wise," the philosophers' stone of remarkable properties. Jung has shown us [28] that the alchemists projected upon the materials on which they performed chemical experiments the unconscious transformation process of the psyche. The gold or miraculous metal which the alchemists sought to produce corresponds psychologically to the self or the whole man, and the dominant symbols of the alchemical process, Jung has shown, are symbolic attempts to unify the opposites in human nature.

There is a striking correspondence between this dream and the psychological meaning of alchemy. In seeking to relate the opposites in himself the dreamer had unwittingly become a psychological alchemist. This was far from his mind at the time of the dream; he knew nothing of alchemy, he was only in search of healing. Like someone drilling for water and finding oil instead, who becomes unintentionally the owner of an oil well, so our dreamer went into himself, and became unintentionally the inheritor of the psychological work which the alchemists carried on more or less unconsciously hundreds of years ago.

It is from the collective unconscious and particularly its store of alchemical symbols that we come to understand this metal which the dreamer realizes he has within his grasp. The alchemists spoke of this metal as a "living thing," a material substance imbued with a spiritual life. It was both the beginning and the end of the alchemical process. As the beginning, it set in motion the alchemical work; as the end of the process it was the living substance which drew all things unto itself in remarkable unity. In the dream this symbolism is further strengthened by the shape of the metal, which is cubic, and so expresses totality by its equidistant sides, and by its magnetic quality which attracts things to its positive and negative poles.

We can also find parallels to this symbol in Christian tradition. In the Bible Christ is several times described as the "living stone." In I Peter we read, "Come to him, that living stone, rejected by men but in God's sight chosen and precious." [29] And St. Paul writes of the Israelites in the wilderness, "For they drank from the supernatural Rock which followed them, and the Rock was Christ." [30] Of the magnet, St. Augustine writes: "We know, that the magnetic stone in a wonderful manner draws iron unto itself, which caused a cold shudder in me the first time I saw it." [31] The dreamer had this same feeling of the wonderful and awful nature of what he was confronted with. We find much the same symbolism in the Eucharist. Here the opposites of spirit and matter are united in the substance of the bread and wine. The earthy, material substance becomes endowed with the spiritual reality of Christ, thus uniting the opposites in one symbol, just as there is a living spirit in the magnet, so is there a living spirit in the eucharistic substance. Like our dreams and alchemy, the Eucharist is also a work of God and man, something which requires human effort and concentration. Indeed, the very word "liturgy" means the "work of the people."

Symbolically, the living metal of the dream parallels the symbols of alchemy and certain Biblical images. Psychologically, it corresponds to the advance of the dreamer towards his own psychic center, where diverse things are drawn together. He has this center, so to speak, in his grasp, as a living thing which he can approximate conceptually and so keep hold of.

[*192*]

The meaning of the magnet as a symbol for the psychic center also accounts for the effect which this dream had upon the dreamer. The dreamer regarded this dream as "dreadful" and "wonderful"; it left him with a feeling of awe which he says remained for a long time afterward. The emotions of awe, dread and wonder are the religious emotions par excellence; they make up the feeling of numinosity which characterizes religious experience, as Rudolf Otto has shown us in his masterful book *The Idea of the Holy*. The Bible is filled with the record of such numinous experiences, as for instance, in Jacob's dreams, Abraham's encounters with the angels of the Lord, Moses' confrontation with God in the burning bush, Ezekiel's visions which left him almost paralyzed for seven days, Isaiah's and Jeremiah's calls to their ministry, and in the New Testament the experience of the Transfiguration, Saul's vision of Christ on the road to Damascus, and so forth.

In dealing with unconscious material we often encounter this feeling of numinosity, for instance when we meet the archetypes, or when we are confronted with the symbols of the self. Something numinous can also adhere to persons and things when we project upon them archetypical qualities. I recall a woman who consulted me for some time. She used to speak of a trembling emotion which overtook her entering my office and of the electric atmosphere which she felt my office had. Actually, there is no electricity in the atmosphere of my office, but there is such electricity, or numinous power, in the psyche of this woman. Wherever the self appeared in our consultations, she felt this power arising between us. To the extent to which counselor and counselee are unconscious of the religious significance of this numinosity as a radiation of the self, it may be taken for sexual desire. But when we understand that the power of the experience, and the fantasies which often are connected with it are energies of the self, released upon the union of opposites, then we may use such experiences to come closer to a confrontation with God. The numinous feeling our dreamer felt with regard to the magnet shows the possibilities for a religious experience which occurs when dealing with the symbolic relationship between the magnet and the psychic center.

If it seems strange to the reader that in a 20th-century man's dream the Christlike, reconciling symbol should be visualized as a living metal, let me remind him that Christ has not always been treated in our present matter-of-fact way. In the Bible, as we have noted, he is compared to many images, such as that of the "living stone," or a "consuming fire," [32] a sacrificial Lamb,[33] a living bread and water,[34] a door or way,[35] a thief in the night,[36] a serpent on a cross,[37] and so forth. And in early Christian life He was represented as a fish, lion, eagle, lamb, the sun, and the phoenix, to name but a few of His symbols. Only in recent centuries have we lost our ability to come closer to unknown spiritual realities through symbolic expression. Our dreams continue to speak in such images.

Nor should it seem unreasonable to see the center of personality in such an image. To be sure, the workings of the unconscious are strange, so the symbols it uses to depict these workings are also often strange. But how else could such a center show itself than through symbols and images? And what image could better express the balanced power of the unity of opposites than our dream's image of the magnetic, living metal? In the image of the equal-sided cube we have expressed the idea of totality; in the image of magnetism we have the thought of the center as something which exerts an attracting force on diversities within personality. The image of something alive within a material substance conveys the "spooky" reality of a human being, whose material body and brain pulsate with spiritual life. Like the dream symbol, we too are matter with a living spirit. At first glance it seems like an unlikely symbol; upon reflection, it would be difficult to imagine a symbol which would express more simply such a paradoxical reality.

It is easy to follow the inner development of these dreams. First there is the implacable split of the opposites and a fierce struggle for the supremacy of one side. Then there is hope: negotiations are taking place, but the "devil-man" seems determined to go on with his rebellion. But by this time, the dreamer has hold of something, and the astonishment of the devil-man shows that this something will completely change the inner situation. In the third dream, the dreamer senses what it is that he now grasps: it is the mysterious goal, the magnetic metal, the reconciling, uniting center of personality which offers him the possibility for wholeness. It is the psychological reality corresponding to the theological figure of Christ the God-man.

These dreams also show us the nature of the inner work. It requires both consciousness and the unconscious. The ego must accept the ferocity of the inner struggle, must brave the dangers of hell, and must persevere in the face of intense discouragement. But the final solution is a gift from God, not from a human source. The miraculous metal was not made by consciousness, but came as a gift from the unconscious depths. So our dreams strive to compensate our one-sided attitudes, and to bring us close to the experience of inner release and reconciliation which underlies the Christian experience.

Conclusion

Man's oldest problem is the problem of opposites. It is the problem par excellence of both psychology and religion. It is one of the basic problems with which the Bible deals. It is *the* basic problem the psychotherapist or priest of the soul confronts today.

We began by showing how the problem of opposites had torn asunder a contemporary Christian. For this is no abstract philosophical problem, but an everyday problem for everyone to solve. Then we saw the problem in the Bible, where the answer was found in the figure of Christ. But this answer was too paradoxical for men to understand; they were not ready for it, so men recoiled from the saving symbol of Christ and the Cross. The unconscious, because of its highly compensatory character, tends to bring us closer to this forgotten paradoxical solution of the conflict. This we saw illustrated in a series of three dreams of a healing process resulting in contact between the ego and the reconciling, paradoxical center within the psyche.

God is present in the depths of man's being. This is why the psyche is so creative and continuously in the service of higher consciousness and development. For God is first and foremost a Creator. The conflict of opposites in our world today is a desperate one, but because of the creativity of the unconscious depths there is room for hope. But alas: we Christians all too often reject the very psyche through which God speaks. Dreams illuminate the problem of the opposites, and help us to become aware of the irrational, paradoxical center of personality which can bring healing and regeneration. But we all too often cast aside, despise, reject, and fear the very dreams through which God speaks.

We say we do this because the unconscious realm from which dreams come is dark and evil. The reason for its darkness is simply that we have banished all our darkness into its depths. We don't recognize our unfairness; we act as if we would not know that the unconscious is dark only because we have forced it to absorb all that is dark in us. Nor do we recognize the absurdity of thinking we can escape the problem of our shadow by closing our eyes. We refuse to accept the lesson of history and psychotherapy, that a man does not eliminate the devil by refusing to talk with him, but only gives him the capacity to become really satanic by banishing him from his consciousness, and allowing him to act autonomously.

So here is the tragedy: we are cut off from a possible solution to our most pressing problem because we have cut ourselves off from the unconscious part of our psyche. In so doing we have shut ourselves off from the Voice of God in our dreams though it offers us—as it were—continuous redemption. The reconciliation of the opposites, and the acceptance of the unconscious as a psychic principle of equal importance with consciousness, is the basic Christian problem.

Centuries ago the prophet Isaiah, foreseeing the glory and peace which would come with such reconciliation, wrote of the divine child who was to be the Messiah:

The wolf shall dwell with the lamb,
   and the leopard shall lie down with the kid,
and the calf and the lion and the fatling together,
   and a little child shall lead them.
The cow and the bear shall feed;

their young shall lie down together;
and the lion shall eat straw like the ox.
The sucking child shall play over the hole of the asp,
and the weaned child shall put his hand on the adder's
den.
They shall not hurt or destroy
in all my holy mountain;
for the earth shall be full of the knowledge of the Lord
as the waters cover the sea.[38]

So shall it be when Christ is born in man, and man once
again becomes whole, and so expresses God.

IX

The God Within

Let us, like mountain climbers, pause a moment and survey the distance we have come. We began our discussion of dreams with some actual case histories. In Chapter I we saw how dreams helped lead Tom out of a seemingly impossible situation by bringing him to the kind of self-confrontation which is integral to the religious life. Chapter II described how Margaret was enabled by her dreams to find the solution to the difficult religious problem of forgiveness. In Chapter III we discovered indications from dreams that there is a dimension of reality which is beyond space and time, and a meaningful example was cited of a dream which suggested a life beyond death. In Chapter IV we saw how dreams may attempt to slice through the conventional, prejudiced thinking of our age in order to reconnect us to a living spiritual world. In Chapter V, we began to deal with the delicate question of what a complete or whole person might be like.

Beginning with Part Two, we noted the central place which dreams occupied in the religious experience of the men of the Bible, and in passing called attention to the similar importance of dreams in the life of the early Church. There followed a chapter on the general nature and structure of dreams which led to the discussion of one of the oldest spiritual problems of man: how to deal with the opposites in ourselves in order to find wholeness. We saw dreams which described the emergence of a psychic center where opposites were paradoxically united. We drew comparisons between this uniting center of personality and the Christian understanding of the reconciling nature of Christ. The close connection which exists between dreams and man's central religious problems seems to justify our calling dreams "God's forgotten language."

But how can we substantiate so intimate a relationship between our dreams and God? In a way this can be done simply: our dreams are the voice of the psychic center within us which enables us to strive for wholeness. This psychic center can be characterized as reconciling and Christlike. Experiences with this center belong among the highest ones in human life; men have always called them experiences with God.

But this simple formulation of the relationship between dreams and God raises some questions. What further comparisons can we draw between the activity of the self and traditional Christian theological formulations? And most important of all, granting that our dreams are the voice of the self, or the image of God within us, does this also mean that they represent the metaphysical God, the God whose Reality transcends the capacities of the human psyche? Let us begin by distinguishing as carefully as possible between the self, the psychic center, or God within, on the one hand, and God as a transcendental Reality on the other hand; an Existence which would continue even if all humanity were to perish, an Eternal Existence beyond our concepts.

Who is God? No man knows. He is Existence; He is Life; He is the Ground of all that is. But who He is in Himself, no man can say. In the words of the Bible, "No man hath seen God." [1] Yet the idea of a divine being is as old as man's history, and it is a psychic fact that man has

always considered himself influenced by deity. Although
we cannot prove God directly, we do have an idea of God
which is not consciously fabricated but is derived from an
unconscious source. Jung has shown that this unconscious
source is describable as a psychic center, and he gives it the
name of the self. In thinking about what psychology has to
tell us about God, we must make a careful semantic distinction between God as Ultimate Reality and the self, or inner
image of God, existing in our psyche.

We may assume, but cannot prove, that the inner image
of God corresponds to the actual reality of God as He
reveals Himself in the universe. To use an imperfect example: my church recently built a new building. Before the
building was started the architect constructed a model. By
looking at the model of the building people could get an
idea what the building would look like. But the model was
not identical with the building itself, even though it was an
accurate representation. Now in the psyche there is what
we can call a "model of God." Jung calls it the self, and
describes it as an inner image of God. We described some
of the functions of the self as reconciling and balancing the
qualities of personality. We can say that the self is the
archetype of wholeness and meaning. The activity of the
self, or of the God-image within us, necessarily gives rise
to the idea of God in our conscious minds, for unlike the
static model of the building the self is energetic and active.
But does the self or inner God-image correspond to what
God might actually be like in His absolute, transcendental
sense? This question psychology cannot answer.

When Jung speaks as a psychologist about God, he is
describing the God-image in the psyche. He is not making
metaphysical statements but is asserting the empirical fact
that man's unconscious psyche contains an image of God

which is transmitted to consciousness through dreams and other psychic experiences and produces the idea of God. Imagine that we were fishing at a lake and that in this lake there lived a huge but rarely seen fish, which dwells at great depth, troubles the water and threatens to overturn our small boat. We would no doubt become greatly interested in this fish and we would conceive all sorts of ideas about it. In some such way does the God-image live and move in the psyche and give rise to conscious ideas about God. It effects religious experiences, in which our personal identity seems to merge with a reality far beyond itself, an *unio mystica* with God.

In his later writings Jung sometimes expresses his personal conviction that God is a transcendent God, as well as a psychological reality. But speaking as a psychologist he is careful to stress that when he speaks of "God" he is not making metaphysical statements, but empirical ones. He writes:

> When I say as a psychologist that God is an archetype, I mean by that the "type" in the psyche. The word "type" is, as we know, derived from "typos," "blow" or "imprint"; thus an archetype presupposes an imprinter. Psychology as the science of the soul has to confine itself to its subject and guard against overstepping its proper boundaries by metaphysical assertions or other professions of faith. Should it set up a God, even as a hypothetical cause, it would have implicitly claimed the possibility of proving God, thus exceeding its competence in an absolutely illegitimate way. Science can only be science; there are no "scientific" professions of faith and similar "contradictiones in adjecto." We simply do not know the ultimate derivation of the archetype any more than we know the origin of the psyche. The competence of psychology as an empirical science only goes so far as to establish, on the basis of comparative research,

[202]

whether for instance the imprint found in the psyche can or cannot reasonably be termed a "God-image." Nothing positive or negative has thus been asserted about the possible existence of God, any more than the archetype of the "hero" proves the actual existence of a hero.[2]

Dr. Gerhard Adler, a psychotherapist who lives in England and is a student of Jung's, puts it this way:

> This fact of the existence in the psyche of an archetype which man has termed "God," and its actualization through the impact on the conscious mind, takes us to the end of our empirical and psychological statements. All that we can say, strictly speaking, is that religion is a fundamental activity of the human mind, and that there exists an archetypal image of the Deity deeply and indestructibly engraved in our psyche. Psychology cannot prove or disprove the existence of God; what it can prove, however, is the existence of an archetypal image of God, the "self." Here, then, psychology and religion both part and meet, facing each other from different sides of the frontier. All that psychology can legitimately do is to look across and accept the possibility that the "God within us" corresponds to a transcendental reality.[3]

The God-image in the psyche is a living, energic reality. The self may be said to generate psychic energy, to be a center for the psyche, and to give a direction to psychic development. We can liken the self to a spiraling circle in the psyche. It is the circumference which includes all psychic energies and potentialities within itself; it is also the center of the circle, to which all things within are related; it is furthermore the movement of the spiraling circle which gives it direction. For this reason the self often appears in dreams symbolized by a circle, or a concentric mandalalike design. But at other times it can take on the appearance of a

symbol filled with energy, such as fire or wind or a whirling cyclone; or a great dynamism like a huge beast or an
engine. Students of the Bible will be familiar with similar
images of God from the Bible, where God is pictured as
fire, wind, whirlwind, fiery chariot, a being surrounded by
whirling wheels, or as a flaming torch. Psychologically
these symbols express tremendous psychic energies, their
essential unity, and their purposeful movement.

When we grasp that the psyche contains this energy-
filled image of God we begin to understand why the men
of the Bible and of the early Church felt dreams to be
expressions of the Deity. For our dreams express these psychic inner energies; they relate us to the center of these
energies, and they place us in contact with a kind of unconscious direction which these energies serve. In short, our
dreams express the Mind of God within us. This understanding also leads us to a comprehension of certain things
in the development of religion, and to further interesting
comparisons between psychology and traditional Christian
theological formulations.

Consider polytheism as an example. Man's belief in many
gods, goddesses, demons and spirits was grounded upon the
complexity of the psychic forces within himself, which
were projected outside of him in personified form. So real
were these psychic realities that the Fathers of the Church
never denied their existence. The Fathers simply made it
clear that what the pagans took to be gods were in fact
demons; lesser psychic powers not meriting worship but
nonetheless real.[4] For instance, consider the goddess Aphrodite. A man falls in love. This has the effect of releasing in
him an unexpected flow of energy and passion which was
not previously felt by him consciously but was in an unconscious, latent state. He is no longer the same man as he

was but is transformed. Because ancient man knew he was not the master of this new emotion, but rather it mastered him, he quite reasonably felt himself affected by a divine being, and in the case of the Greeks he named her "Aphrodite." We now can say in view of modern psychology that it is his anima who infuses him with this feeling, and floods him with this new energy. But a rose by any name smells just as sweet, and has just as many thorns! Or take the idea of a demon. The ancients would see a man possessed by something which infuses him with a violent energy, and destroys his ability to control himself. Anyone could see at a glance the man was possessed by a power superior to that of his ego. This superior, possessing energy the ancients called a "god," in this case a "demon god." Today we would say the ego is possessed by an autonomous complex, a buried complexity of emotion, which suddenly erupts to engulf the ego.

How about monotheism? Monotheism corresponds to man's realization that the inner powers which affect him are essentially a unity. When man thinks he is just the victim of countless unrelated forces, then he is a polytheist. But when he realizes that his life experience, and his inner energy or libido have an essential unity, in spite of their seeming multiplicity, then he becomes a monotheist. Thus monotheism is a tremendous religious progression over polytheism, because it enables man to come closer to his wholeness.

There is an interesting parallel between the psychological image of God and the Christian concept of the Trinity. We have already described the image of God as the primal source, the center, and the directing mover of the energies of the psyche. Yet these are not three energies but one. Now Christian theology teaches: God the Father, God the Son, God the Holy Ghost, three persons in one God. The

[*205*]

first is God as Creator, the second is God as expressed in the person of Jesus Christ, the third is God as working now in the world of men. God the Father we can know psychologically as "God" the primal source of our psychic energies. Here in the depths of the psyche is where a power "moves over the face of the waters" and brings our psychic world into existence, including the ego.

Theologically God the Son is God Incarnate in Christ the God-man. Psychologically God the Son is "God" as expressed in man; hence the Son corresponds psychologically to the center of the psyche where the wrathful, conflicting energies of the personality are reconciled and united. When St. Paul says, "Not I, but Christ who lives in me," he means that his ego is no longer trying to be the center of his life, but that his life and energies are related to a new center, which he now knows is living in him. Through our Christlike center our whole self may be realized, and God and man, the unconscious powers and the human ego, can be united.

Finally, God as the Holy Ghost corresponds psychologically to that which we sense subjectively as the purposive nature of the unconscious energies within us. The Holy Ghost is an active agency at work in men, seeking to realize God's deepest purposes, to bring men to their Christlike center. "When the Spirit of Truth comes. . . . He will glorify me, for he will take what is mine and declare it to you." [5] Our dreams serve this task as they lead us to our own center, and so are a classic example of the work of the Holy Spirit.

Our psychological language may be new, but such a perception of God as a force within man's own soul is nothing new in Christendom. It is an ancient, neglected way of looking at the meaning of Christianity. Hundreds of years ago the great Christian mystic Meister Eckhart wrote: "I have said it often: There is a force in the soul. God himself is in this force, unceasingly glowing and burning with all his splendour, bursting forth in a continuous, unspeakable ecstasy of joy." And again, "God begets his only Son now and in all eternity within every honestly watching soul. . . . Everything that God the Father has ever given to his only begotten son in human nature, he has also fully given it to me. Nothing is excluded: neither wholeness, nor holyness; he gave me all, as he gave him all." [6]

The Christian Father Hippolytus writes in a similar vein:

For thou hast become God: for whatever sufferings thou didst undergo while being a man, these He gave to thee, because thou wast of mortal mould, but whatever it is consistent with God to impart, these God has promised to bestow upon thee, because thou hast been deified, and begotten unto immortality. This constitutes the import of the proverb, "Know thyself," for He has formed thee after his own image. For with the knowledge of self is conjoined the being an object of God's knowledge, for thou art called by the Deity Himself. [7]

St. Augustine puts it very clearly:

And we indeed recognize in ourselves the image of God, that is, of the supreme Trinity, an image which, though it be not equal to God, or rather, though it be very far removed from Him—being neither co-eternal, nor to say all in a word, consubstantial with Him,—is yet nearer to Him in nature than any other of His works, and is destined to be yet restored, that it may bear a still closer resemblance. [8]

It is not too much to say that the life process which psychology perceives at work in us, and which Jung calls "individuation," is the restoring of the image of God within us to "a still closer resemblance."

But what about Satan? In the Bible Satan emerges as a figure personifying those destructive influences at work in the world which seem to thwart the will of God. It is not hard to see the relationship between this theological idea and the psychological fact that man's nature includes a whole host of demonic passions and emotions which all too easily can possess or destroy the ego and bring the whole process of wholeness to ruin. "Satan" psychologically is the personification of those collective forces in man which seem to be demonic. When during World War II man's greed, power drive and brutality possessed his mind and perpetrated horrors upon the world, we could have aptly said, "Satan did it," so long as we remembered that this Satan is in us. Any emotion or passion, or any lower motive, which comes to possess a man's ego to the extent that the man is cut off from his center and the positive forces within him are excluded from expression, is the work of Satan.

At one time Christians felt that Satan worked primarily through those human passions which tempted man to murder or adultery or some sin of passion. No doubt at one time it was man's inability to gain control over such powerful impulses which threatened his development and so was Satan for him. But now, I would submit, the situation is different. That which primarily thwarts the work of God in man is man's own unconsciousness of himself. If man looked at what was within himself he might come to terms with the devilish impulses. Spiritual sloth and its ally, egocentricity, are our worst enemies today. What works against the purposes of God is man's blindness to himself, his unconscious and prejudiced condition which causes him to deny his soul and therefore readily succumb to the demonic.

[*208*]

The question of the relationship between Satan and the Trinity is the famous question of the "3 and the 4," the relationship of darkness and the divine which has so concerned Dr. Jung.[9] In most theological thinking God and Satan have nothing to do with each other, although we still insist upon a complete monotheism in which God is responsible for everything. The philosophical difficulty of such a position is apparent. What is not so apparent is the series of psychological problems which result from this theology.

It is interesting that in the Bible this absolute split between God and Satan was not always so distinctly drawn. At one time the image of God in the Bible contained both good and evil. When, for instance, Saul is angered at David, the First Book of Samuel tells us, "an evil spirit from God rushed upon Saul." [10] Later, in the book of Isaiah we read, "I form light and create darkness, I make weal and create evil, I am the Lord, who do all things." [11] Abundant other verses in the Old Testament, some of them quite late, show a similar affinity between god and evil in Jahweh.[12]

We have not space in this book to elaborate in detail the progressive differentiation of Satan from God. It culminates in the Book of Revelation, where Satan is firmly and irrevocably split off from the good side of God: from Christ. Psychologically speaking, the development of the relationship of Satan to God in the Bible corresponds first to man's growing conscience, which increasingly differentiates between good and evil, right and wrong, and secondly to the extreme difficulty men have always had integrating the dark, demonic potentialities of their inner energies into their conscious life. For this is a task which demands moral decision in order to make sense.

Most of us would feel more comfortable if we could ascribe only goodness to God and leave evil to Satan. But unfortunately, we have split Satan off too much from the image of God. By so doing we have opened ourselves to periodic victimization by the dark powers, left in an unconscious, autonomous, unrelated condition. As we saw in the previous chapter, the integration of the dark polarity within man is the great problem of our time. Perhaps we must first integrate the dark powers into our conscious image of God if we are to succeed in integrating ourselves. Certainly the symbols of the self which come from the unconscious depths include a dark element in their image of totality.

In spite of the seemingly irrevocable opposition between God and Satan, it still remains true that without Satan man's ego could never become sufficiently conscious and differentiated to recognize and to express the God within. Without the serpent in the Garden of Eden man would have remained a moral idiot; without evil in the world today most of us would be blissful, comfortable, spiritual imbeciles. Who knows, perhaps when the final curtain goes up at the end of the drama we will discover there was a secret alliance between God and Satan all along, and that the goodness of God is far greater than the good and evil we human beings distinguish in this world.

To return to our main theme: in our dreams the whole host of the spiritual world lives on. Demons and angels, Satan and the spiritual forces of God, all the psychic world of the first Christians, are recreated for us nightly. But ultimately our dreams are in the service of wholeness, and of the psychic center of the personality. When understood and acted upon,[13] our dreams help us establish a conscious relationship to this inner image of God. In this way they are the Voice of God.

But the question may be raised: dreams are so often filled with that which is dark and sinister; how can this all be God's voice? It often seems more like the devil's!

[*210*]

There is no doubt that our dreams can express the darkest and most sinister thoughts, impulses and events. We saw such sinister dreams for instance in the case of Tom, where the motif was one of violence and murder, and where the unconscious situation the dream expressed was actually producing a serious impairment to health. The same holds true for the first two dreams of Chapter VIII, where the dreamer was compelled to wrestle with a highly dangerous adversary. Our dreams can show us murderous thoughts, temptations to become involved in illicit sexual affairs, and contamination with all manner of demonic impulses. Worst of all, dreams sometimes portray psychic situations which are heartrending because of their hopelessness. It is particularly agonizing to come across dreams of children in which desperate psychic situations are expressed.

Nevertheless, we should not blame the dream for the sinister things which can happen in the psyche. The dream does not cause these sinister fates, it just expresses them. Now anyone can see that human beings are exposed to dangerous and destructive psychic influences. A child may become so injured through deprivation of love, parental conflicts, or a variety of diseases that his life prognosis becomes well-nigh hopeless. But such evil is a fact of life which cannot be avoided. Our dreams, being faithful to life, express the evil which exists. No matter how negative the dream may seem, it in itself is not evil. It only seeks to express the evil, making it possible for it to be identified by consciousness, in order that the process of healing can be set in motion.

Jung's understanding of God as a psychological reality and our ability to describe some of the psychology which lies behind the inner God-image has helped us to define more closely what we mean by saying that the dream is the language of God. We have also noted that Jung, speaking purely as a psychologist, does not deal with the existence of a transcendental God beyond the human psyche. Is there such a transcendental God? If all human beings perished, would God die? Can our dreams be said to express the reality of a transcendental God as well as that of the inner God-image?

It will do no good to try and ignore the issue. The question whether or not there is an Ultimate Meaning to the universe is one which every human being must ask himself. So far in this book I have spoken largely from an empirical point of view, basing what I have had to say on observable facts about the human psyche. But here is a question science cannot answer, so I speak now as a plain man and as a priest. For me it is unthinkable that there should not be an Ultimate Reality behind the psychic image of God in our minds. Through the God in the psyche there is mediated the Will and Energy of the Creator Himself. When our life expresses a purpose which moves us, it also expresses the purpose of the entire Creation. Through realizing the self in a way which can be grasped psychologically, we also relate to the transcendental Christ of history. I cannot prove these statements, of course, for our science is not able to go beyond the observable facts of this life. But I do claim that he who knows and has been affected by his dreams will feel in himself a thread of meaning and purpose which is part of something much bigger than himself. This is the faith which lives in me.

If this faith corresponds to reality, then our dreams, which are the voice of the living God within, are also connected to the transcendent God who is behind all of the universe. If the opposite were true, then we human beings and our marvelously constructed psyches, with their creative energies, reconciling center, and seemingly purposive direction, would only be a fantastic accident in a meaningless universe. It cannot be that there is meaning to an individual human life but no meaning to what is beyond individual life. So it cannot be that there is a God and meaning within our life as a psychological fact, but no God and no meaning behind all life. The dreams, which express the basic, psychologically verifiable reality, must also be connected—in ways as yet beyond our scientific knowledge—to the Ultimate Reality.

Because I feel that there is an essential identity between the God-image in the psyche and the final order of the universe, or the transcendental God, I see in the workings of the unconscious a call to cooperation with the purposes of God wherever they can be recognized. This is certainly a calling to cooperation with the self, to the search for the wholeness of our personality, and to the anchoring of our life in a greater psychic reality than that of the ego. We are called upon not only to seek God, so that He may be realized in us, but also to help our fellow men to a realization of God in their lives.

No one can approach his own wholeness without realizing his commitment to his fellow men, and to what God is seeking to realize in them. The apostles regarded themselves not only as men who sought and found their own salvation in God, but as men called upon to communicate to others the meaning of God's work. For after all is said and done, we see in the psychic center a reconcilement and creativity which must be described as a manifestation of love, and love cannot be fulfilled without reaching out to include others in its circle. The self, then, which seeks to bind the opposites in us together in a unity, also seeks to bind us in unity to our fellow men.

[*213*]

Man is not only conscious; he is also unconscious. Unconscious psychic reality is as real and substantial as is our conscious life. It expresses its reality in a hundred ways; one of which is the dream. The center of our conscious life is the ego, the center of our total psyche is the self, which seeks to express through our consciousness the totality of our nature. The experience of the totality of our nature is not *just* a psychological experience, but also a religious one in the sense that it connects us with a meaning and purpose beyond our egos. Our dreams serve our psychic totality, and seek to bring the ego into relationship with the psychic center in order that our totality may be consciously known and lived. So our dreams serve the God within, and act as one manifestation of His voice to man.

The experience of God, psychologically speaking, is the experience of the depth, the height, and the unity of our own psyche. The search for God is the search for this depth and height of our being, for the complete Christlike man who is waiting within us to be consciously realized and expressed in our human relationships. We could call this search for God also a search for self-realization. But we must be careful not to confuse such self-realization with the realizing of limited, ego purposes. The ego is not to cultivate its own purposes only, but also the deeper purposes of the larger personality within us. We are not the masters, but the servants of the God within. Anything short of this understanding of the humble, though vital, role of the ego in this self-realization runs the danger of disastrous inflation. This occurs when the ego consciously or unconsciously identifies itself with the psychic center and so tries to assume a Godlike role. Examples of this God-identification are apparent in various forms of insanity, and in history, for example, in the case of Adolph Hitler. Such identification is possible because of the close relationship between the ego and the psychic center, a relationship which is at the heart of religious experience.

It is understandable why the world has chosen to ignore so studiously the inner reality of God, for dealing with God can be a frightening experience. Understanding God as the inner source of our life and energies, as one who speaks through our dreams, our relationships, and the events of our life, brings Him entirely too close for comfort. It is much more comfortable to leave God to theologians and take care of our anxieties by taking pills and blaming our neighbors for our distress. The self makes enormous and frightening demands upon consciousness. If we ignore these demands, the energies of our soul may become wrathful. Then "Satan" persuades us to remain unconscious and to hope that God will go away.

But behind all of that which we fear from our unconscious world there is a great love; a love which pours forth out of our own soul. But this love of God is so intense and so demanding that we hesitate to enter into relationship with it.

I have tried to state the psychological meaning of God in a few, clear statements. But the realizing of God's effect in us is not so simple. Jung devoted his lifetime to the description of the process by which the whole man in us is realized. He calls this process "individuation." Complete and complex as his description is, there remains much more to be discovered: realizing our psychic totality is a task of a lifetime. The moments of religious insight when for an instant we know ourselves to be utterly, wonderfully whole are the rare exceptions. Furthermore, realizing our psychic totality is not something we accomplish in isolation. The life of the whole man will necessarily involve us in the lives of our fellow men and in the conflicts of our time. Throughout this process of realizing the whole man in us, we will be vexed by the need for a continual and painful surrender of our egocentricity. For this is not a process which the ego commands, but which it serves; the conscious mind must accept, and consider, the higher authority of the self. Our dreams are the voice of this higher authority: the God within. And if this God is identical with the final order and meaning of the universe, then our dreams express the will of the transcendent God as well.

NOTES

Chapter I

1. Gen. 32:22 ff.

2. The words "and with men" in verse 28 are thought by scholars to be a later addition to the original text.

3. Some people complain that they cannot remember their dreams. This can be overcome by keeping pencil and paper handy at the bed and immediately upon awakening attempting to note what of the dream comes to mind. When one still is unable to remember a dream, there may be various reasons: fear of something unconscious, lack of a relationship with someone with whom such things may be discussed, or half-conscious prejudices against "vagaries" may play their part.

4. See Dement's article in the *Journal of the American Psychoanalytic Association*, April, 1965.

5. For instance, this interesting passage from the extant writings of Julius Africanus, Eerdmans series, *The Ante-Nicene Fathers*, Vol. VI, p. 128. Regarding an early Christian legend of Christ's early manifestation in Persia, we read this ancient Persian legend which was likened to Christ: "This stream of water sends forth the perennial stream of spirit, a stream containing but a single fish, taken with the hook of Divinity, and sustaining the whole world with its flesh as though it were in the sea." Another example is drawn from the Acts of Andrew and Paul, the apocryphal story in which the Christ Child catches 12,000 fish, who follow him about on dry land. Certainly the symbolism of Christ as a Eucharistic fish was prevalent by the 2nd century. As an underwater creature which can be caught and brought up into the light, the fish is a natural symbol for living unconscious contents, which likewise can be "caught" and brought up into consciousness.

Chapter II

1. Isa. 1:18.

2. As psychoanalysis, i.e., Freud and his school, meant it.

3. C. G. Jung, *Memories, Dreams, Reflections*, Pantheon Books, p. 14.

Chapter III

1. Matt. 17:2.
2. Prentice Hall, New York.
3. Our conventionally disciplined minds are tempted in the face of such dreams to reject them entirely, and lay them at the feet of deluded mentalities. Certainly we must recognize the extreme difficulty we will encounter if we try to treat such dreams in the usual scientific way. Nevertheless, is it not much more unscientific to reject them on the a priori grounds that "such things cannot be"? Only a bogged-down consciousness would say so, for such statements accord poorly with the world of creation.
4. I Cor. 13:12.
5. John 3:8.

Chapter IV

1. John 3:3–5.
2. The reader must not confuse "collective thinking" with the collective unconscious of which we have spoken before. The latter is the Universal Unconscious, sometimes called the Objective Psyche, which is common to the psyche of all men and is the repository of our ancestral experiences and of our urge for the future. Collective thinking, on the other hand, (Jung calls it "Collective Consciousness") is something which grips and possesses our *conscious* minds. Because the terms are easily confused, I will frequently use the term "mass thinking" as an alternative to "collective thinking."
3. I Pet. 5:8.

Chapter V

1. I will use the terms "center" and "self" interchangeably. "Self" is the term Dr. Jung coined, though he also spoke of the "center." I prefer "center" since it is more descriptive and less likely to be confused with such terminology as "himself" or "herself," etc.

Chapter VI

1. Num. 12:6.
2. Matt. 1:20.
3. Matt. 2:12.
4. Matt. 2:13.
5. Matt. 2:19.
6. Matt. 2:22.

7. When Matthew simply says "an angel of the Lord said in a dream. . . ." we need not suppose that a vision of a stereotyped angel appeared and quoted those words. An "angel" was a "messenger." The dream *is* the message, and the "angel" is the direct source of the dream. What the actual dream might have been we have no way of knowing. All we have is the interpretation that such and such was meant.

8. Luke 1:22.
9. Luke 24:23.
10. Acts 10:3.
11. Rev. 9:17.
12. Ezek. 8:3; also 11:24; also 40:2.
13. II Cor. 12:1 ff.
14. Acts 2:17.
15. I Sam. 28:6.
16. I Sam. 3:1.
17. I Chron. 17:3 and 17:15.
18. Ps. 89:19.
19. Hos. 12:10.
20. Gen. 46:2.
21. Acts 9:10.
22. Acts 10:9 ff.
23. Acts 16:9.
24. Acts 18:9.
25. Num. 12:8.
26. Jer. 23:16; see also Jer. 23:25 ff; 27:9; 29:8–9, and Deut. 13:1.
27. Gen. 15:12–13; 17–18.
28. Gen. 20:3.
29. Gen. 28:10–12.
30. Gen. 37:5, 8–9, 11.
31. Gen. 40:5 ff.
32. Gen. 41:16, 25.
33. Job 4:12–17.
34. Job 33:12–18.
35. Job 7:11–14.
36. Ezek. 1:1.
37. C. G. Jung, *Psychological Types*.
38. The symbolism of numbers in general, and of four in particular, did not escape the attention of the Church Fathers. St. Augustine, for instance, after describing the importance of the number six, writes, "And, therefore, we must not despise the science of numbers, which, in many passages of holy Scripture, is found to be of eminent service to the careful interpreter" (*City of God*, Bk. XI, Ch. xxx). Irenaeus, *Against Heresies*, Bk. III, Ch. xi, Art. 8, stresses the religious importance of the

four. See also the fragment "On the Creation of the World," by the early Christian martyr Victorinus.

39. Ezek. 1:12 and 14.
40. C. G. Jung, *Flying Saucers: A Modern Myth of Things Seen in the Sky.*
41. Song of Sol. 3:1–5.
42. *Song of Sol.* 5:2–8.
43. Dan. 1:17.
44. Dan. 2:1.
45. Dan. 2:18.
46. Dan. 2:19.
47. Dan. 2:27–30.
48. Dan. 2:31 ff.
49. Dan. 4, 10–17.
50. Dan. 4:19.
51. Dan. 4:25–33.
52. Dan. 4:34.
53. Dan. 4:27.
54. Judg. 7:13–14.
55. Judg. 7:15.
56. I Kings 3:5.
57. I Kings 3:15.
58. Matt. 17:9.
59. Acts 26:12 ff., especially verse 19.
60. Matt. 27:19.
61. Heb. 10:31.

Chapter VII

1. For further details on this subject see the April, 1965, issue of the *Journal of the American Psychoanalytic Association.*
2. C. G. Jung, *Über Psychische Energetik und das Wesen der Träume*, Zürich, 1965. S. 123.
3. Plato, *Phaedo*. Benjamin Jowett translation, *The Portable Plato*, pp. 195–196.
4. The Bible contains many exceptions. Since its major concern is not with individual psychology but with the events taking place in the nation of Israel and the Church, it naturally includes more dreams of general interest than we would expect to find in the typical dream collection.
5. Tertullian, *Apology*, Ch. xvii.
6. But note that the identity is not complete. The "dream ego" may know things unknown to the conscious ego. There is a similarity, yet a mysterious difference, between the two.

7. Matt. 13:45–46.

8. Gen. 32:22–30.

9. Job 4:12–16.

10. C. G. Jung, *The Structure and Dynamics of the Psyche,* Vol. 8, *Collected Works,* pp. 149–151.

11. It is sometimes said that Jung's patients dream "archetypal" dreams because they know this is what Jung is looking for and they want to please him, so, obligingly, they manufacture this kind of dream. Actually such dreams are commonplace and may be found from many sources which have nothing to do with Jung. Consider the following example taken from the book *Children of Sanchez* by Oscar Lewis, Vintage Books, 1961, p. 108. Lewis, a sociologist, records verbatim the autobiographical accounts of several poor Mexican children. One of them, Consuelo, spontaneously reports her dreams, including this one of her father: "This time in my dream my father had moved the bed and the shelf of the saints to a different wall. Manuel and Roberto were in the bedroom, Marta and I in the kitchen. One of the panels of the bedroom door was only half-closed and I looked in. I saw my father leaning over the bed, holding in his hands a heart, the heart he had torn from the body of a young painter, Oton, who lived in the same tenement. Oton was lying on the bed, face upward. I could see the cavity from which his heart had been torn. My father was holding the heart high and offering it to somebody. I had a terrible fright and awoke with the same cry I always make when I dream. I have never been able to get rid of the sight of my father holding that bloody heart in his hands." The comparison between this dream and the ancient Aztec ritual in which the heart of a prime, living victim was flung to the Great Goddess is unmistakable.

12. See also E. Neumann, *Ursprungsgeschichte des Bewusstseins,* Zürich, 1949.

Chapter VIII

1. In a way this is a deceptive name, for a "tiger" in the language of the unconscious would indicate a devouring instinctive quality. Nevertheless, because of the peculiarly rapacious quality of her collective conscious attitudes, which seemed to always demand "being fed," this is the name we happened upon and continued to find ourselves using.

2. Nikos Kazantsakis, *The Last Temptation of Christ,* p. 15.

3. Gen. 1:26–27.

4. Gen. 2:7.

5. Gen. 3:5.

6. Gen. 3:10–11.

7. Gen. 8:21.

8. Ex. 15:26.

9. Jer. 23:5–6.
10. Joel 2:1–2.
11. Isa. 53:3.
12. Luke 14:26.
13. Matt. 12:46 ff.
14. Cf. Matt. 10:37 ff., Mark 10:29 ff., Luke 8:19, Luke 2:43 ff.

15. So we read in the Acts of Andrew, "Hail, O Cross, yea be glad indeed! . . . I know thy mystery, for the which thou art set up; for thou art planted in the world to establish the things that are unstable, and the one part of thee stretchet up toward heaven that thou mayeste signify the heavenly word, and another part of thee is spread out to the right hand and the left that it may put to flight the envious and adverse powers of the evil one, and gather into one the things that are scattered abroad. And another part of thee is planted in the earth, and securely set in the depth, that thou mayest join the things that are in the earth and that are under the earth unto the heavenly things. . . . O cross, planted upon the earth and having thy fruit in the heavens! O name of the Cross, filled with all things." (M. R. James, tr., *The Apocryphal New Testament*, p. 359–360.) Cf. Irenaeus, *Against Heresies*, Bk. V, Ch. xvii, Lactantius, *Divine Institutes*, Ch. li, and Hippolytus, *Treatise on Christ and Antichrist*, par. 4.

16. Rom. 7:15 ff.
17. Paraphrase of Rom. 6:3–4.
18. Gal. 2:20.
19. I Pet. 3:11.
20. I John 1:8–9.
21. Rev. 19:11–15.
22. Rev. 20:15.
23. Matt. 11–19.

24. A particularly glaring example among many others may be found in the 158th letter of St. Augustine in the first volume of his writings, p. 510. Eerdmans series, *The Ante-Nicene Fathers*.

25. See Chapter I.
26. Gen. 15:17 ff.

27. The fact that the dream referred to both protagonists as "sons" reminded the dreamer of the elder and younger sons in the parable of the prodigal son.

28. C. G. Jung, *Psychology and Alchemy*.
29. I Pet. 2:4.
30. I Cor. 10:4.
31. St. Augustine, *De Civitate Dei*, Bk. XXI, Ch. v, Art. 4.

32. Heb. 12:29. See also the apocryphal saying of Jesus, "He who is near to the fire is near to me." Gospel According to Thomas.

33. Rev. 5:6 ff.

34. John 4:14, 6:35.
35. John 14:6.
36. I Thess. 5:2.
37. John 3:14.
38. Isa. 11:6–9.

Chapter IX

1. John 1:18; I John 4:12.
2. C. G. Jung, "The Religious and Psychological Problems of Alchemy," introduction to Psychology and Alchemy, Vol. 12, *Collected Works*.
3. Gerhard Adler, *Studies in Analytical Psychology*, Routledge & Kegan Paul, Ltd., 1948, pp. 162–163.
4. See for instance: Eusebius, *Church History*, Bk. X, Ch. viii, Art. 10; Lactantius, *Divine Institutes*, Ch. vii, Dionysius of Alexandria, extant fragment "From the Books on Nature," Ch. iii; Justin Martyr, *First Apology*, at end Ch. v; Tertullian, *Apology*, Ch. xxiii.
5. John 16:13–14.
6. Meister Eckhart, *Vom Wunder der Seele*. Reclam Verlag, Stuttgart, 1959, Sermons and Writings 60, 68 and 72. I thank my good friend George Doczi of Seattle, Washington, for calling my attention to these words of Meister Eckhart's, and for their translation.
7. Hippolytus, *Elucidations*, Ch. xxx. Hippolytus (A.D. 170–236), Bishop of Portus, was a disciple of the great Catholic theologian Irenaeus of Lyons.
8. St. Augustine, *City of God*, Bk. XI, Ch. xxvi.
9. See especially C. G. Jung, *Aion: Researches into the Phenomenology of the Self*, Vol. 9, Pt. 2, *Collected Works*.
10. I Samuel 18:10.
11. Isa. 45:7. The Revised Standard Version uses "woe" instead of "evil," an indefensible translation of the Hebrew "ra," especially since elsewhere the R.S.V. almost invariably translates "ra" as "evil." We must assume that this error comes from the subjective prejudice of the translators that God cannot be thought to be the author of evil, a prejudice not shared by the Old Testament.
12. Cf. Job 2:10; Amos 3:6; Joel 2:13; Ex. 4:24 ff., Ex. 33:12 ff.
13. "Acting upon" a dream means allowing ourselves to be changed in such a way that the larger personality our dreams reveal will be expressed in our life. Wholeness is not a static condition, a closed circuit within the psyche, but an activity which must be lived to be realized.

Our dreams seek to lead us to a kind of inner wholeness. But if we are to truly realize this inner wholeness it must be expressed in our outer life of work, relationships, love and commitment.